Language, Social Class, and Education

Of course Glaswegians cannot be expected to be totally objective about the city in which they dwell. But, of all cities, Glasgow generates a fierce pride and sense of belonging among its inhabitants, and this alone should make passing observers worry about making hasty judgements about either Glasgow's citizens or its environment, parts of which may seem unpromising to the outsider.

Glasgow Herald 11 May 1973

D0709716

Language, Social Class, and Education

A Glasgow Study

R. K. S. MACAULAY
with the assistance of G. D. Trevelyan

Edinburgh
University
Press

© R.K.S. Macaulay 1977
Edinburgh University Press
22 George Square, Edinburgh
With the financial assistance
of the Scottish Arts Council

ISBN 0 85224 320 0

Set by Speedspools, Edinburgh
Printed in Great Britain by
Morrison & Gibb Ltd
Edinburgh

Contents

CONCORDIA UNIVERSITY LIBRARY
PORTLAND, OR 97211

Preface

The present volume is a considerably revised version of a report to the Social Science Research Council on a survey of language, education and employment in Glasgow, which was supported by the Social Science Research Council, the Scottish Council for Research in Education, and the research and development committee of Pitzer College. The original report (Macaulay and Trevelyan 1973) has circulated in a number of versions and material from it has appeared in several articles: 'Negative prestige, linguistic insecurity, and linguistic self-hatred', *Lingua*, *36*, 1975, pp.147–61; 'Linguistic insecurity', in *The Scots Language in Education*, edited by J. D. McClure, 1975, pp.35–43 (Aberdeen: Aberdeen College of Education); 'Social class and language in Glasgow', *Language in Society*, *5*, 1976, pp.173–88; 'Tongue-tied in the Scottish classroom', *Education in the North*, *13*, 1976, pp.13–16; 'Variation and consistency in Glaswegian English', to appear in *Sociolinguistic Patterns in British English*, edited by P. J. Trudgill (London: Arnold). I am grateful to many people for their comments on these articles and on the original report and I have incorporated many of their suggestions in this revised version.

First of all I am greatly indebted to Jack Aitken for his continued support and encouragement and for his critical reading of the text. His comments have been consistently perceptive and constructive, and my only regret is that I was not able to take advantage of them at an earlier stage in the analysis. Next I wish to thank Gavin Trevelyan for his work both on the survey itself and in the preparation of the original report. He not only wrote the section on the city itself (chapter 2) but contributed in many ways to the writing of the original report. I would not have been able to complete the work by the deadline without Gavin's help and I remain sincerely grateful to him. The phonological analysis described in chapter 4 is based on the work of Valerie Waggott and Elaine Holder, and the analysis of intonation in the same chapter was carried out by Dr Wiktor Jassem of the Polish Academy of Sciences. To all three I am greatly indebted. Peter Trudgill, Bob Berdan, Dell Hymes, Bill Labov, and Suzanne Romaine have all helped me to see things in the data that I would otherwise have missed.

Numerous other people contributed to the survey itself in a number of ways. Mr James J. Bain, Director of Education for Glasgow Corporation, gave permission for me to visit the schools and interview teachers and pupils. Miss Elizabeth McKechnie,

Advisor in Speech and Drama, Glasgow Education Department, saved the project from disaster several times by her advice and assistance in locating schools. Mr Thomas Logan, Secretary to the Appointments Board at the University of Glasgow, was similarly helpful in making contacts with employers. Mr Laurence Iles, Mr David Cruickshanks and Mr Ronald Motherwell were of inestimable help by making it possible for the survey staff to use the facilities of the Phonetics Laboratory at the University of Edinburgh. Professor M. L. Samuels provided an academic base at the University of Glasgow by having me seconded to his department as a research scholar during the period of the survey. Dr W. B. Dockrell made the whole project possible by supporting the application to the Social Science Research Council and by being generous with the resources of the Scottish Council for Research in Education. Mr William Hogg's contribution went far beyond his efficient administration of the budget. Dr H. H. Speitel of the Linguistic Survey of Scotland and Miss Janet Templeton of the Department of English Language, Glasgow University, supplied useful comments and welcome encouragement. Finally, I am indebted to the head teachers of the schools I visited and to all the informants, whose names are omitted in the interests of anonymity but without whom there would be nothing to report. To all of the above I wish to record my sincere gratitude.

R. K. S. Macaulay, Pitzer College, California

1. Introduction

> Language is an all-pervasive characteristic of the individual such that he becomes a verbal organism, whose walking, eating, love-making, and the rest are altered in keeping with his symbolic experience. . . . Language transforms experience first by creating new channels through which the human environment can act on the child. . . . At the same time, the learning of language transforms the individual in such a way that he is enabled to do new things for himself, or to do old things in new ways.
>
> Joseph Church (1961, 94-95)

THIS IS A book about language, in particular about variation in language and the social significance of that variation. It is only an apparent paradox that all human beings are very similar as regards their use of language and at the same time very different from each other. It all depends upon the perspective. If we see a crowd of figures in the distance we may only be able to identify them as human beings; as we get closer to them we can see that they consist of old and young, men and women, and other such categories; eventually, if we examine them closely enough we shall find that no two are exactly alike. The same is true of language. Although linguists have made only slight progress in isolating linguistic universals, it is clear that all human languages share many common features of organization, a fact that helps to explain the extraordinary ability human infants possess for learning the particular language they happen to be exposed to at the critical time. As we look at languages more closely, however, we also find groups of speakers whose linguistic behaviour is similar enough for us to consider them 'to be speaking the same language', although if we look closely enough we shall find that no two speakers are exactly alike in their knowledge and use of 'the language'. The aim of this book is to investigate neither the universal nor the individual aspects of language. Instead, it deals with the characteristics of language shared by groups of speakers, groups determined by such shared attributes as age, sex, and social class, since one of the ways in which people show their membership in a particular group is by the way they speak.

The way someone speaks is similar, in certain respects, to his choice of clothes and style of haircut. Both speech and physical appearance provide advance information about an individual's age, sex, prosperity, and meticulousness, among other things. Such

1

an observation needs no detailed study to support it, since it is part of the everyday knowledge of ordinary members of the community. However, what is usually lacking is precise information about the basis of the judgements made by members of the community. In the case of clothes and hairstyles the absence of detailed information may be unimportant, partly because fashions in such matters change quite quickly and apparently unpredictably. With speech the situation is very different. Many forms of speech survive more or less unchanged for remarkably long periods of time and when they do change it is likely that particular social pressures have contributed to the change (Labov 1963; Trudgill 1972, 1974).

To take an example that is relevant to the present study, in most parts of the English-speaking world the word *house* is pronounced [haʊs], although there are numerous small variations in the quality of the diphthong [aʊ]. However, in many parts of Scotland the pronunciation [hus] may be heard and if age conferred respectability this would be the 'correct' pronunciation of *house*, since a pronunciation of this kind goes back long before Chaucer's time, back even to the period before English was a separate language. The change of pronunciation from [hus] to [haʊs] probably took place some time between Chaucer's death and Shakespeare's lifetime, though the exact date is hard to establish. However, in some parts of the country, particularly in Lowland Scotland, some speakers did not adopt the new pronunciation and retained the older one. It is this traditional pronunciation that has survived for a number of Scots, if not as their only form of *house* then at least as an alternative to [haʊs].

The survival of the pronunciation [hus] in spite of all the pressures towards conformity with Southern English, since the eighteenth century at least, might seem surprising. It is possible that in all schools in Scotland for more than a hundred years the pupils have been encouraged to say [haʊs], not [hus], and nowadays the latter pronunciation is rarely heard, for example, on the radio, on television, or in the church. Yet the use of [u] for [aʊ] in a large number of words has survived, and there are no reasons to believe that it is likely to disappear in the near future. This survival is a striking example of the resistance of a section of the community to the pressures of conformity. Part of the motivation for the present study comes from a desire to investigate the complex conditions that produce such remarkable effects. Linguists frequently study linguistic change, but an equally interesting phenomenon is linguistic stability or resistance to change.

This is also a book about education and the role of language in education. The importance of language in education can hardly be exaggerated. Not only is language the medium through which

2

education is conducted in talking, listening, reading, writing, analysing, organising, inferring, comparing, and so on, but also a great deal of what is learned through education is language itself: new words or expressions, more precise meanings of familiar words and expressions, different ways of describing familiar objects, and so on. However, although the exact nature of the effect of family background and linguistic differences on educational achievement is still a matter of dispute (Bernstein 1973, Labov 1969, Trudgill 1975), it seems to be the case that the language the child uses may seriously affect his chances of success in the educational system (Bullock 1975). The present work does not attempt to investigate this question directly through comparing the child's use of language with his academic progress; instead, it explores how attitudes towards language contribute to the linguistic environment in which the child finds himself, to the way in which he is treated in the school, and how he reacts to that treatment.

The survey on which the present work is based consisted of three sets of interviews tape-recorded in Glasgow between March and June 1973. The first set of interviews was with a cross-section of the population of Glasgow in order to obtain a varied sample of speech within the community. The second set of interviews was with teachers at primary school, secondary school, training college and university. The third set was with personnel managers and others responsible for interviewing job applicants. The results, discussion and conclusions presented in the chapters that follow are based on the analysis of the tapes of the interviews.

This work, therefore, deals with the speech of one area, the city of Glasgow, a city that has been frequently criticised and seldom defended, at least by those who do not belong to the city. 'For the hopeful voyeur of sheer obscenity in modern urban life, Glasgow is hard to beat', wrote a reporter in *The Guardian* (8 May 1973, p.18). The speech of Glaswegians has likewise been condemned: 'There are few to sing the praises of the accent . . . of Glasgow' (Harvey 1968, 12). It is probably not a coincidence that a city that is seen as ugly and violent should be judged to have an accent that is ugly and rough. The two perceptions are consistent with each other, but they are the judgements of outsiders. The study that is reported in the following pages is an attempt to investigate the attitude of Glaswegians towards the speech of their fellow-citizens, by examining what they say and how they react to some examples of Glasgow speech. It is also an attempt to describe some features of pronunciation in Glasgow and discover to what extent an individual's age, sex, social class, and religion affect the way he speaks.

The present study cannot claim to provide a complete picture of the situation; that would have taken more time, skill, knowledge, and resources than were available. The compromises that were adopted as a consequence of the speed with which Time's winged chariot brought the deadline rapidly nearer are fully discussed elsewhere.[1] However, there is one limitation on the nature of the evidence collected in the survey that is so fundamental that it must be mentioned here. The study of pronunciation presented in chapter 4 is based on examples of speech collected in the formal interview situation. Thus it is no guide to the kind of speech used in other situations. It is well known that style of speech varies with the situation in which the speaker finds himself, and one has only to walk around Glasgow for a few minutes to overhear examples of styles of speech that are unrepresented in the interview materials. The reason for the absence of such styles in the interview situation is that they are not considered appropriate for such a situation. In his autobiography, Clifford Hanley (1958, 19) puts the point very succinctly:

> We ourselves grew up trilingual. We spoke the King's English
> without any difficulty at school, a decent grammatical informal
> Scots in the house, and gutter-Glasgow in the streets.

It would have been ideal to investigate the extent to which this 'trilingual' situation still exists, but the problem of collecting systematic evidence of different situation-based styles presents a challenge to the sociolinguistic investigator that cannot be successfully taken up in a short space of time. Regrettably, the Glasgow speech described in this report must be considered to come under the heading of 'the Queen's English', 'Standard English', 'school English' or any other similar label that would indicate that the informants, conscious of the formal interview situation with an unfamiliar interviewer and all too conscious of the presence of the tape-recorder, were using their 'best' English. In spite of this limitation, the range of pronunciation represented on the interview tapes is extensive. Moreover, the differences in pronunciation are related to age, sex, and social class. This in itself is hardly surprising but what may come as a surprise to some people is the accuracy with which an individual's speech reflects his position in society (see chapter 4). This has been demonstrated before, most notably in New York (Labov 1966) and in Norwich (Trudgill 1971), and the results from the Glasgow survey are consistent with those in the earlier studies.

What is perhaps the most important difference between the present investigation and earlier studies is the emphasis in the Glasgow survey on attitudes towards speech. This was in an attempt to explore the conflict expressed by a working-class man

[1] See Macaulay and Trevelyan 1973, 221-31.

in one of the exploratory interviews carried out in 1970:

'I suppose like – when – especially when you're on TV – ye hear Scots folk – sounds terrible ye know – but, uh, I don't think I'd like to speak any other – than the way we do speak.'

Similar sentiments were expressed by a number of informants in the present survey, including teachers and employers, and these attitudes are discussed in chapters 7 and 8. The attention devoted to attitudes towards speech in the present survey indicates the importance we believe such attitudes to have in the urban language situation. Many of the teachers and employers interviewed believe that the substantial differences in the speech of individuals do not necessarily reflect differences in linguistic ability, yet many decisions on whether to employ someone or not are taken on the basis of an interview. If the evidence of the interviews with the employers is even partially correct there would appear to be too many Glaswegians who may have suffered economically, not through lack of ability or knowledge, but through a failure to realise the importance of the impression made when being interviewed for a job. There is also some evidence that the teachers are not always aware of this either. It is not the intent of the present work to dictate to teachers, employers or ordinary citizens what they should do about this situation, but instead to draw attention to the picture that emerged from the three sets of interviews, so that they can make their decisions in the light of this evidence.

It may be thought by some people that this book is overly concerned with pronunciation or accent, a matter that any reasonable person ought to treat as of minor importance. Pronunciation is, however, literally superficial; it is the most easily observable aspect of linguistic behaviour, and this fact has significance both for the investigator of linguistic situations and for the member of a speech community. It is significant for the investigator because it is much simpler to collect evidence of variation in pronunciation than it is to investigate grammatical or lexical differences. However, it is also important for the ordinary member of the community because snap judgements about an individual's ability or personality may be made on the basis of such superficial characteristics of language. The investigation of pronunciation is preliminary to a systematic investigation of more important differences in language but that study must be left to a future survey. The present work is not presented as a definitive account of the linguistic situation in Glasgow. On the contrary, it is merely a first, tentative approach to a very complex situation. The most that can be claimed for the present survey is that it may help to correct some misconceptions about the linguistic situation in Glasgow. As is so often the case, the greater part of the task remains to be done.

5

At the same time, the implications of the findings extend far beyond Glasgow. As will be discussed in chapter 10, the problems of educational failure and the role of language in that failure are of great concern throughout both Britain and the United States. It is very likely that the situation found in Glasgow will have its parallels in many other locations and for this reason it is hoped that the conclusions of this study will be of interest to linguists and educators generally, not only to those who are interested in Glasgow. The report of the Bullock Committee (1975, 514) states as one the recommendations:

> Each school should have an organized policy for language across the curriculum, establishing every teacher's involvement in language and reading development throughout the years of schooling.

The chapters that follow make it abundantly clear that the development of such a policy will be no easy task, since the linguistic behaviour of human beings is remarkably complex and highly resistant to pressures to change. However, it is in the hope that a better understanding of this complex situation will lead to the emergence of an organised policy for language in the curriculum that this present work is submitted.

2. Glasgow : The Setting

In Glasgow there are over a hundred and fifty thousand
human beings living in such conditions as the most bitterly
pressed primitive in Tierra del Fuego never visioned.

Lewis Grassic Gibbon

PRESENT-DAY GLASGOW is a city that was shaped by the
Industrial Revolution and that is now still trying to disentangle its
nineteenth-century social problems and find for itself a twentieth-
century industrial base. Between the last decades of the eighteenth
century and the first decades of the twentieth, Glasgow was a boom
town: it went through several stages of commercial and industrial
growth, which made it prosperous enough to establish its own
banks, and it increased in population from 40000 to just over a
million people. At that time the living conditions of a large part of
the working population were as bad, if not worse, than any other
industrial town in Britain, but still people continued to pour into
Glasgow and the town continued to thrive.

But after the boom that followed the First World War, Glasgow
went into decline. The unemployment rate rose, and in the 1930s
almost a third of the working population was unemployed. Glasgow became a depressed area. The population became static at
around the million mark, since what births added to the population
was lost in emigration. However, the city was still overcrowded by
modern standards. Population densities in parts of the city were the
highest in Britain, and the Clyde Valley Regional Development
Plan (1946) proposed that 300000 people be moved out of Glasgow
to bring the population down to 700000. The same plan proposed
to bring new industries to Glasgow so that the city should be re-
habilitated economically.

Situation

The city of Glasgow, on the west coast of Scotland, forms part of
the central Clydeside conurbation, which is set in the Clyde River
basin. This basin is elongated in shape and is hemmed in to the
north by an encircling upland of hills and to the south and east by
swampy ground, which gives limited access to the lowlands. These
geographical features inhibit the spread of the Clydeside conurbation.

The conurbation is densely populated and covers an area fifteen
miles long by ten miles wide (figure 1). It contains a high proportion

7

not only of central Scotland's, but of the whole of the country's population. There are little short of two million people living in this urban agglomeration, which is just over one third of Scotland's population. (Contrast this with London's eleven per cent of the total population of England and Wales.) The concentration and fusion of these tightly packed communities has resulted in a great urban growth of practically continuous built-up areas, centred on the main block of Glasgow. But because of the way the area has already been developed and because of the nature of the basin in which it is situated there is little room for development.

Glasgow itself has a population of 896000, which is half of the population of the Clydeside conurbation. The concentration of

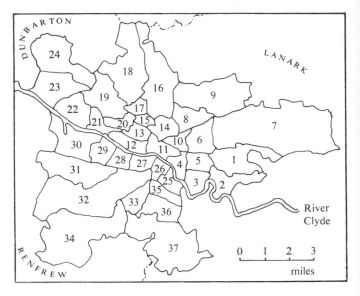

1. Shettleston &	13. Park	26. Gorbals
Tollcross	14. Cowcaddens	27. Kingston
2. Parkhead	15. Woodside	28. Kinning Park
3. Dalmarnock	16. Ruchill	29. Govan
4. Calton	17. North Kelvin	30. Fairfield
5. Mile-End	18. Maryhill	31. Craigton
6. Dennistoun	19. Kelvinside	32. Pollokshields
7. Provan	20. Partick East	33. Camphill
8. Cowlairs	21. Partick West	34. Pollokshaws
9. Springburn	22. Whiteinch	35. Govanhill
10. Townhead	23. Yoker	36. Langside
11. Exchange	24. Knightswood	37. Cathcart
12. Anderston	25. Hutchesontown	

Figure 1. The city wards of Glasgow

people is such that the city has twice the population of Edinburgh, capital of Scotland, yet covers an area the same size as the capital.

Growth of Glasgow

The main period of growth of the city was the nineteenth and early twentieth century. From 1765 to 1801 the population more than doubled from 28000 to 77000; from 1801 to 1901 the population grew tenfold from 77000 to 762000, and by 1911 it had topped the million mark. The cause of the enormous concentration of population in Glasgow was the commercial and industrial activity on the west coast at this time, which was centred on Glasgow. It was the colonial trade and the industrial revolution that made Glasgow. The city, and the region, went through four distinct phases of economic growth.

After the Act of Union (1707), which united Scotland with England for the first time, Scottish merchants could legally participate in trade with England's colonies. Glasgow was curiously favoured for trade with the American colonies, situated as it was on the western seaboard with the shortest distance across land in the whole of Britain to ports on the eastern seaboard. This gave Glasgow the advantage for goods in transit from the Americans to Europe. Glasgow became the centre of the tobacco trade and her merchants prospered by it.

However, the colonial wars in the middle of the eighteenth century caused a slump in the tobacco trade, and when the colonial trade was re-established cotton replaced tobacco as the staple import. By the end of the eighteenth century the manufacture of cotton goods had replaced that of linen. The west coast of Scotland became one of the centres for the new cotton industry. Hand spinning and weaving gave way to new mechanical methods, cottage industry to the prototype factory. Early in the nineteenth century this use of machinery in the factory system caused the formerly dispersed textile industry to be concentrated in urban centres. By 1841 the influence of the cotton industry on the city was complete. The early use of steam power in Glasgow attracted a large number of the mills there, and in this way Glasgow's supremacy was established.

From 1830 onwards, however, cotton, as the main cause of industrial growth and population expansion, gave way to the exploitation of the local coal and iron resources. These new processes were associated with a phenomenal growth in urban population, particularly in the mid-Clyde valley. The ironworks and blast furnaces were concentrated in the eastern outskirts of the city and along the Monkland Canal, particularly around Coatbridge. This turned old, small settlements into new growth points. In contrast, the rate of growth of the old textile area to the south west of the city was very much slower. This era also saw a similar growth of urban areas in the Ayrshire coalfields.

The last phase of industrial growth came towards the end of the century. There were new developments in ship building and marine engineering in the 1870s and 1880s, which established the Clyde as the leading centre of the shipbuilding industry in Britain. In 1901 it was claimed that within the previous thirty years the Clyde had built more famous vessels of the highest class than probably all the other shipbuilding rivers put together. In addition to the passenger ships and cargo ships for use for trade and transport in the different parts of the British Empire, the shipyards in Glasgow also built naval vessels. This was the start of the period of the naval race between Britain and her European rivals, and the Clyde was constructing warships of many kinds. Up to and during the war, the naval requirements greatly inflated the amount of work done in the Clyde shipyards.

By the end of the century Glasgow had also become the third largest British port by net tonnage, after Liverpool and London. The first of the tidal docks, the Kingston Dock with five acres of water space, was opened in 1867; the Queen's Dock, with thirty-four acres, in 1880; the Prince's Dock, with an even larger water space, in 1900.

Up to and during the First World War great demands were made of Glasgow's shipyards and other industries. There was a short period of expansion after the war when international trade was set going again. But the Clyde shipbuilders soon found their industry in decline. There were no more government orders and the continent and Japan began to rival Britain as shipbuilders. The production of iron fell from 760 000 tons in 1913 to 18 000 tons in 1927, picking up again for a short time in 1928 to 600 000 tons and falling again in the thirties to 56 000 tons in 1933.

The pattern shown in Glasgow was common to other centres of heavy industry in Britain. After a short post-war boom, business became chronically depressed. In 1921 approximately two-and-a-half million people were out of work. During the twenties the figure did not fall below one million, and in the thirties the figure had risen to almost three million.

In Glasgow between 1923 and 1939 the level of unemployment was always more than ten per cent. In the years around 1932 the figure had risen to thirty per cent. In fact, between the wars Glasgow was a depressed area in need of special attention, and almost a third of its citizens were in a distressed state. These were the hard years, which Glasgow has still not forgotten.

During the Second World War the Clyde Valley Regional Plan (1946) was drawn up to see that the same thing did not happen to

Glasgow again. While the main idea behind the plan for Glasgow was to ameliorate social conditions, it was understood that this had to be linked with industrial development. Efforts were to be made to attract new industries to the region. Changes in employment structures have now meant that employment is highest in distributive service and professional areas. However, the main industries in Glasgow are still the shipyards, engineering works and steel furnaces.

In the nineteenth century Glasgow was called 'the Second City', for it was the second largest city in the British Empire. By 1951, however, Glasgow was the third largest city in Britain, Birmingham taking second place. However, on the 1944 figures, Glasgow had an average gross residential density of population two-and-a-half times that of Birmingham. This reflects the relatively small acreage on which Glasgow is built, particularly the smaller percentage of land that is occupied by housing, and also reflects the way in which the population was housed in the nineteenth century.

The housing shortage created by the rapid growth in population in the nineteenth century was met by building tenements, a style of building that came to Scotland from Central Europe. These tenements were sandstone buildings, four storeys high, which contained units of one, two, three or more rooms. Thus, even when the buildings were put up, a large number of them were overcrowded by modern standards. However, the tenements were so sturdily built that they continue to stand. Except for the detached houses in the wealthier suburbs, all the housing built in the nineteenth century was of the tenement type. In 1880 it was estimated that one quarter of Glasgow's population was living in single room dwellings, and only eight per cent of the population lived in houses of more than five rooms.[1]

The increasing population densities of the mid-nineteenth century led to the first slum clearances, in the 1860s. In that decade a City Improvement Act was passed by Parliament, which called on the Town Corporation to clear parts of the city in which people lived at a density of 1000 per acre. In 1889 seven more congested areas were cleared. For the last twenty-five years housing has been considered to be a major problem in Glasgow because of the high densities of population in certain areas and because of the type of housing that people occupied. Since the war the Glasgow Corporation has been tackling the problem of housing intensively.

A picture of the city in 1951 showed three levels of population density. The less densely occupied core of the city was on the north

[1] In 1951 about half the dwellings in Glasgow were of one or two rooms. Nearly a quarter of the whole population were living more than two to a room.

bank of the river and had a population density of 30.49 people per acre. This was the shopping and commercial centre of the city, with a relatively small residential population. The inner zone, the inner decaying city, stretched on both sides of the river and completely encircled the inner core. In this area lived nearly sixty per cent of the city's population at average gross densities of 50–120 people per acre, with a maximum of 145.4 in the Gorbals and 158.8 in Woodside. The bulk of the older and poorer blocks of tenements, together with a high proportion of the city's industrial concerns, was concentrated in this area. In most wards a third, and in Hutchesontown up to seventy per cent, of the houses had no bath and no separate internal lavatory. The third zone, suburban Glasgow, had not only much lower residential densities, less than thirty people per acre, and a larger proportion of open spaces, but consisted of newer and better dwellings. About forty per cent of the city's population lived in this zone, to the north and south of the city.

Since 1911, when private investors stopped putting money into rented housing stock because of the lack of profit in it, the onus of providing accommodation in Glasgow has fallen on the City Council. Up to now the Corporation has built 105 000 houses, and owns one third of the housing stock in Glasgow. These 105 000 Corporation houses are contained in thirty estates, or 'schemes', as they are usually called, situated principally on the northern, southern and eastern boundaries of the city. (The four main schemes are Castlemilk, Drumchapel, Pollock and Easterhouse.) Half of these houses were built before the war and the other half in an intensive period of building since the war. In the latter period 150 000 people have been moved from the congested inner city to the new estates on the outskirts. This dispersal of people has meant a great change in life for those who have been shifted. They have been moved from overcrowded houses in highly populated city areas out to flats or bungalow-type houses in much less densely occupied 'garden' suburbs; street communities, which often meant related families as well as friends, have been broken up and the people transferred to different schemes. When the schemes were built houses came first, and shops, schools and other facilities were added later. There was virtually no entertainment on the schemes – no cinemas, no pubs – and this, besides the fact that neighbourhood communities were broken up when people moved out to the schemes, has been the main complaint about life there.

In the 1950s the Corporation decided not only that they would move people out of the inner city zone, but that the worst areas in the city would be completely redeveloped; the old tenements and industrial buildings would be pulled down and the areas built up

12

again in a modern fashion. At the same time the areas would be repopulated at only forty per cent of the previous densities. The remaining sixty per cent of the old population would have to be rehoused elsewhere. At first five, then twenty-nine, areas in the city were designated redevelopment areas. These twenty-nine areas cover 2700 acres. The first to be approved was the Hutchesontown-Gorbals area, which since the 1930s has had the reputation of being one of the worst areas in Glasgow for social problems. This is, perhaps, why it was chosen as the first redevelopment area, and the way in which it has been redeveloped has set the pattern for other parts of the city.

Included in the redevelopment of these areas has been a modern motorway project, an inner ring road. The boundaries of seven areas were readjusted to include substantial parts of the inner ring road. It was believed that the ring road would help by-pass the city centre and therefore stimulate the development of the offices and shops on the fringe of the city. The western and northern parts of the inner ring road, which includes a new bridge across the Clyde, have now been completed.

In this way it was hoped that Glasgow would be well on the way to securing a more modern centre than any other British city, and that these facilities would increase its attraction for industry and other employment. However, the city itself has not been able to cope with the transferral of population from the inner city zone. This has not been due to a lack of will to build new houses in the peripheral areas, but because by now there is simply no more space to put up more houses at the population densities that were decided on. This has resulted in 'overspill', the movement of population and, where possible, employment out of the city area. The problem was recognised by the Clyde Valley Regional Development Plan, which suggested that 300000 of the city's population should be moved out of the city area, 200000 to be dispersed amongst other towns in the region and 100000 out of the region altogether.[1] Not only has the Corporation contracted with neighbouring towns to take some of the surplus population, but two new towns have been established specifically to help meet the problem. These two towns are in the Clyde Basin; East Kilbride to the south east of the city, Cumbernauld to the north east.

Those who are busy effecting overspill believe that it will take some thirty to forty years to complete and will need cooperation between Glasgow, the new towns and the other towns in the Clyde Basin, but that when it is complete there will be a redistribution of population which will be for the better in the west central region.

[1] So far the population of Glasgow has been reduced by almost 100000.

Social Groups in Glasgow

As has been said, the population of Glasgow grew rapidly in the nineteenth century and the first decade of the twentieth. The incomers to Glasgow were drawn from the west central region, from the Highlands and from Ireland, and this has meant that the population of Glasgow is not homogeneous, but a mixture, in the main part, of people from these areas.

Today the mixture of Scottish and Irish in Glasgow is symbolised by the two religions, Protestant and Catholic. Catholic is taken to denote Irish descent, although Irish people from both the Catholic south and Protestant north migrated to Glasgow. By the middle of the nineteenth century 50000 people were arriving annually from Ireland and this movement of people was at its height after the Irish famine of 1846. In 1878 the Catholic church announced that it believed that Glasgow contained some 450000 Catholics, but that not all of these came from Southern Ireland, some were from Europe. Exact figures for the proportion of Catholic and Protestant in the city are not now known, but figures for attendance at Catholic and non-denominational schools show that forty per cent of the school-going children of Glasgow are Catholics. This would suggest that about two-fifths of Glasgow's population is Catholic, and a large proportion is Irish in origin.

The city itself can be divided up into three socio-economic status areas, and figure 2 shows the situation as it existed in 1966. The classification is based upon that of the Registrar-General, in which classes I and II consist of professional and managerial occupations and class V involves unskilled occupations. The maps are compiled from the 1966 sample Census using districts of the city.

The north-west area contains a high proportion of people in the class I and class II categories and a low percentage of the class V category. This area includes the districts of Knightswood, Yoker, Whiteinch, Partick West, Partick East, Kelvinside, Park Anderson and Exchange. The area to the north and east of the city contains a high proportion of the class V category and a low proportion of the classes I and II categories. This area includes the districts of Maryhill, North Kelvin, Ruchill, Woodside, Cowcaddens, Townhead, Springburn, Cowlairs, Provan, Dennistown, Mile-End, Calton, Dalmarnock, Parkhead, Shettleston and Tollcross. The whole area to the south of the river contains a mixture of the classes. But there are districts in this area which are notably class V in population, those along the south bank of the river: Hutchesontown, Gorbals, Kingston, Kinning Park, Govan and Fairfield. Further out of the city Langside and Camphill have a high proportion of the class I and class II categories.

14

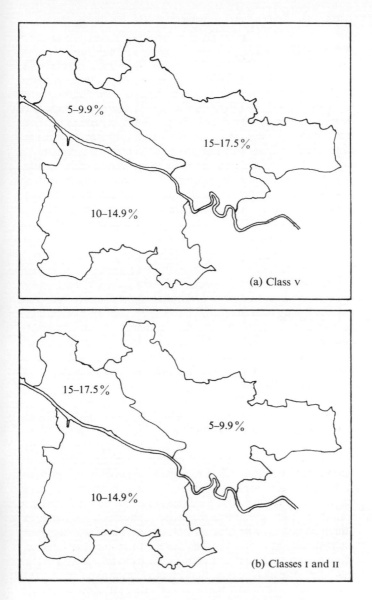

Figure 2. Percentage resident male population of
Glasgow in 1966, (a) in socio-economic class v,
and (b) in socio-economic classes I and II.
(After Dept of Geography, University of Strathclyde,
An Atlas of Glasgow and the West Region.
Edinburgh: Holmes McDougall, 1973)

15

If socio-economic status is related to type of housing, one finds a contrast between areas of the city that include a high proportion of council housing and a relatively high proportion of owner-occupied housing. Three wards, Kelvinside to the north of the city and Camphill and Langside to the south, have about half their dwellings in the owner-occupancy group. Ten other wards have at least thirty per cent of their dwellings in this group. For the most part they embrace the villas and better quality tenement buildings within the city. Conversely the two wards with less than five per cent owner occupancy are Provan (which contains the Easterhouse and Cranhill housing schemes) and Knightswood (which contains the Drumchapel housing scheme). These are virtually entirely post-1920 local authority housing districts. Ruchill and Pollock-shaws also contain a high proportion of council housing. Cathcart ward contains an appreciable number of owner-occupied houses as well as the large Castlemilk scheme.

Social Malaise

Glasgow has a national reputation for slums, social deprivation, unemployment and violence. Although other major industrial cities in Britain have these problems as well, they always appear to be worse in Glasgow. A superficial impression gained from the news media seems to indicate that there are more stabbings, child murders and fatal fires in Glasgow than in any other city. But there are also hard facts about slum conditions and mortality rates, which bear out the impression of the relative harshness of life in Glasgow and the west central region.

The slum conditions in the city have already been noted. To turn to mortality rates, one finds that for women (for the period 1959–1963) Glasgow as a whole had a mortality experience some twenty-five per cent above the national average. Gorbals, Cowcaddens, Kingston, Mile-End and the Calton wards record the highest rates; Kelvinside, Pollockshields, Partick East and Fairfield record the lowest. For men, over the same period, the mortality experience was thirty per cent above the national average. Dalmarnock, Hutchesontown, Mile-End and Kingston wards are the most unfavourable and Pollockshields, Exchange, Kelvinside and Cowlairs the most favourable. Infant mortality rates are also higher than the national average in many parts of Glasgow.

But what commonly draws attention to Glasgow is not the mortality rates, but rather the nature and incidence of violence in the city. Violence in Glasgow means gangs and gang fights, rather than organised crime. Nowadays the gangs are composed of young adolescents and young men between the ages of fifteen and twenty-two, but there are also gangs of younger boys and some girls who

16

are hangers-on to the main groups. The violence takes the form of gang fighting, petty theft and unprovoked attacks on people and property. It is this last aspect of gang violence that has made most people in Glasgow aware of the problem. The weapons that are used by the gangs, besides the chalk and aerosol paint cans for daubing walls with names and gang slogans, are swords and hatchets, razors and knives, bricks, broken bottles and stones, heads, hands and boots.

Gangs in Glasgow are not a modern phenomenon. The social conditions that give rise to the formation of gangs were as much a part of the early development of the city as they are of Glasgow today. In the middle of the nineteenth century organised street fighting was commented on. Men and boys in gangs of up to fifty would meet on the street and fight each other with sticks and stones and they would have to be dispersed by the police. These gangs became part of Glasgow's history and gang law and custom were handed down from those times. Then, as in the gang battles of the thirties, religious differences were an apparent cause of difference. In 1916 there was a serious outbreak of gang violence, which received a lot of public attention. There was much public concern at this time that there were teenage girls who ran with the gangs.

In the 1930s, when one third of the work force was unemployed, gang fighting again became a social nuisance. It is this period that lives in most people's memories and that is contrasted with the present-day situation. Once again the superficial cause of the trouble was religious differences. Sir Percy Sillitoe, who had smashed the gangs in Sheffield, was brought in as Chief Constable to do the same for Glasgow. He broke up the fighting of the most notorious gangs but did not break the gang tradition. Gang lore, if not much gang activity, continued both during and after the war.

When the Govan area was being studied for redevelopment in the 1950s a gang of boys was found whose outlook and activities could only have been derived from the adult generation. When people were moved from the decaying inner city to the new housing schemes on the outskirts of the city, the gang tradition was taken with them and was nurtured in the new areas. There was a resurgence of gang activity in the late 1950s which has lasted up till now. Gangs are found both on the new housing schemes and in the older areas of the city. It is said that gangs have become institutionalised over the years, forming a sub-culture of violence, and certain streets in the city have become synonymous with gang violence. In a recent study of Glasgow gangs (Patrick 1971) more than seventy gangs were noted in the Glasgow area.

3. The Survey

The world is full of obvious things which nobody by
any chance ever observes.

Sherlock Holmes

THE GLASGOW SURVEY consisted of three sets of interviews. The first set was with a sample of native Glasgow speakers
from different backgrounds in order to obtain a wide range of
Glasgow speech, and this will be referred to as the Community
Sample. The second set, with a sample of Glasgow teachers at
primary, secondary and tertiary levels in order to investigate their
opinions about language and the language of their pupils, will be
referred to as the Teachers Sample. The third set took place with
employers, mainly personnel managers of firms within the Glasgow
area, in order to investigate the attention they pay to language in
choosing among job applicants, and will be referred to as the
Employers Sample. The method of obtaining each, and that of
interviewing the informants, will be described briefly below (for
further details, see Macaulay and Trevelyan 1973).

1. The Community Sample

Because it was predicted that language would vary according to
the age, sex, social class and religion of the informant, a quota
sample was chosen to provide an equal representation of both sexes
from three age-groups in four social class categories and with one
quarter of the sample being Catholics. The social class categories
were based on the Registrar-General's classification of occupations:

Class I   professional and managerial (R-G : 1, 2, 3, 4, 13)
Class IIa white-collar, intermediate non-manual (R-G : 5, 6)
Class IIb skilled manual (R-G : 8, 9, 12, 14)
Class III semi-skilled and unskilled manual (R-G : 7, 10, 11, 15)

The reasons for the choice of occupation as the indicator of social
class are discussed in chapter 5. For children, father's occupation
was the basis of selection, and for married women their husband's
occupation, unless the woman herself was (or had been) in an
occupation higher up the scale than her husband's, in which case
her own rating was used.

The sampling method used was based on the need to get an
adequate sample of children. As has been done previously (Trudgill 1974) the sample of children was obtained by going to the

schools. On the judgement of a member of the Education Department a total of seventeen schools, seven primary and ten secondary, including three fee-paying schools, was selected as being representative of the schools in Glasgow. The head of each school was contacted, an interview was arranged to explain the purpose of the survey, and he was asked to suggest the names of children within the school who filled the criteria of age, sex, social class, religion and residence that were applicable at that school. From the names that were suggested at each school one or two children (three at three of the primary schools) were chosen by random choice. In this way thirty-two children, sixteen from each age group, were selected from the schools of Glasgow.

The sample of parents of primary and secondary school children was based on the sample of children that had been selected. Sixteen mothers and fathers, who had been resident from early childhood in Glasgow, were chosen from the parents of the thirty-two children, one parent from every second child.

In each age group there are four Catholics, two of each sex, giving a total of twelve, a quarter of the sample. This is rather less than the estimated forty per cent Catholics in the population of Glasgow, but the size of the sample meant that an exact forty per cent would have unbalanced the distribution through the age-groups. Since religion was not expected to be the most significant extra-linguistic variable, the present compromise seemed preferable to an unbalanced sample.

A list of the informants, showing the socio-economic variables, is given in appendix A.

Interviewing the Informants

Once the names and addresses of the informants, both children and adults, had been obtained through the schools, a letter was sent to the head of each family in cases where only the child was to be interviewed, or to the parent concerned in cases where a parent and a child were to be interviewed, saying that someone would call round to arrange how and where the interview would be conducted, if permission was given. The ostensible purpose of the interview, mentioned in the letter, was to collect information on attitudes towards the changes that have taken place in Glasgow. The informants were not told, either in the letter or when they were contacted, that the primary purpose of the interview was to collect a sample of their speech. The reason for the deception was to avoid refusals and to minimise the self-consciousness of the informants during the interview.

All the interviews were conducted by the principal investigator. The interviews with the adults were conducted in their homes; those with the ten-year-olds and the fifteen-year-olds usually in the schools during class hours. Although the school might be considered the least favourable environment in which to conduct the interviews, the informants did not appear to be adversely affected in their attitude towards the interview. In fact, in a few instances where younger informants were interviewed in the home, the informants seemed, if anything, less relaxed than their counterparts who were interviewed in the schools. Moreover, although the noise level in some schools was quite high, the recording conditions in schools generally compared quite favourably with those in the home, where the extraneous noises were often frequent and unpredictable.

In addition to the recorded interviews, adult and fifteen-year-old informants were asked to respond to tape-recorded examples of Glasgow speech taken from the exploratory interviews carried out in 1970–71. The results are summarised and discussed in chapter 7.

Data Collecting and Analysis

The method employed was basically that of Labov (1966a) in his New York study. The informants in the community sample were interviewed by the principal investigator using a questionnaire designed to elicit continuous speech and to collect opinions on certain topics. A different questionnaire was used for each age group. The questionnaires are given in appendix B.

The method of analysing linguistic variation was also based on that developed by Labov (1963, 1966a), in which a linguistic variable is defined as a class of variants that are ordered along a continuous dimension and whose position on that dimension is determined by some independent or extra-linguistic variable. For example, in Glasgow the pronunciation of the vowel in *hit* ranges from a fairly high front vowel [ɪ] to a fairly low back vowel [ʌ^]. The actual vowel used will depend upon a number of factors including, probably, the age, sex, and social class of the speaker, and also the kind of person he is addressing and the occasion on which he is speaking. By treating this variation as linear it is possible to set up a scale for the variable (i) on which each of the main variants is given a numerical value associated with a point on that scale. The average values for a particular variable can then be calculated for each informant to produce his index for that variable. In turn, the indices for individual speakers can be grouped according to age, social class, sex and religion to discover to what extent the linguistic variation correlates with these factors. The variables chosen for analysis and the results of that analysis are presented in chapter 4.

One major difference between this survey and Labov's New York study is that no attempt was made in the present investigation to isolate contextual styles. Labov was able to analyse his interviews

20

in terms of five different styles:

style A	casual speech	
style B	careful speech	} speaking styles
style C	reading a text	
style D	reading word lists	} reading styles
style D[1]	reading minimal pairs	

Labov made very effective use of the effects of stylistic variation in his analysis of linguistic variables, and his example has set a challenge for all subsequent investigators. Since most people vary their speech according to situation and audience, the question of stylistic variation is clearly one of great importance for the investigator of sociolinguistic phenomena. However, Labov may have been mistaken in claiming that his five contextual styles were on a single continuum. It is reasonable to claim that styles A and B are on a single dimension, namely that of impromptu speech, and that styles C, D and D[1] are on another dimension, namely that of reading aloud. However, there is a gap between the first two and the last three that may be more than a single step, and it would seem advisable to keep the two kinds of stylistic variation separate, since to a certain extent variation in the reading styles may depend on skill in reading aloud. The more important dimension for the sociolinguist is the variation in speaking styles, and the difficulty in collecting evidence of different speaking styles is perhaps the major problem to be faced in a sociolinguistic study. Labov's later study of black adolescents in New York (Labov *et al.* 1968) contrasted group style with individual interview style, and this seems a more promising line of approach than a contrast between speaking and reading aloud.

In the Glasgow survey it was not possible to arrange group sessions because of the limitations of time and resources. Neither did many clear examples of style A, casual speech, emerge in the course of the interviews. Whether this was due to the manner in which the interviews were conducted, the personality and skill of the interviewer, or the attitude of the informants, is hard to determine. Whatever the reason, it would be accurate to describe the speech of the informants in the interview as monostylistic, namely careful, rather formal speech.

Accordingly, in the analysis of linguistic variation in Glasgow, no attempt will be made to deal with the problem of stylistic variation.[1] This limitation is regrettable since, on the surface, the situation in Glasgow presents many examples of stylistic variation, sometimes to a degree that might better be termed code-switching. The exploration of that variation remains a task for a future study.

[1] A brief comparison of reading aloud with the interview style will be presented in chapter 4.

In the present survey the more modest aim of describing the speech of Glaswegians 'on their best behaviour' is presented.

2. The Teachers Sample

The purpose of this sample was to investigate the attitudes of teachers at all levels, primary, secondary and tertiary, towards the speech of their pupils and to discover how much importance they attach to quality of speech.

The informants at the primary and secondary level were contacted through the schools. On the judgement of the same member of the Education Department eight schools, four primary and four secondary, were selected as being representative of the schools in Glasgow (although in this case no private or fee-paying schools were amongst them). One primary and one secondary school were Catholic. The Head Teacher of each school was contacted, the purpose of the survey was explained to him and he was asked to nominate four teachers from his school for interview. The only criteria given to the Head Teacher were that of the four teachers two should be relatively inexperienced teachers and two should be experienced teachers; and for the secondary schools that not more than one informant should be a teacher of English. Four teachers from each of the four primary schools and the four secondary schools were nominated by their respective Head Teachers, making a total of thirty-two informants. Except in the primary school category, equal numbers of men and women were interviewed. The small number of male teachers in primary schools meant that an equal distribution would have severely limited the choice.

The informants at the tertiary level were selected from the two universities and the two teacher training colleges in Glasgow. The informants for the two universities and for one of the training colleges were taken at random from the university and college calendars, those for the other training college were chosen by the Vice-Principal of the college. Four informants were taken from each of the four institutions, making a total of sixteen informants.

The complete list of informants showing sex and the level at which they teach is given in appendix A.

Interviewing

All the interviews were carried out by the principal investigator. All the informants, as well as the Head Teachers, were told what the purpose of the survey was, that the investigator was interested in Glasgow speech and that he wanted to find out what they thought about the language that the children or young adults they taught used inside and outside the educational institution.

The interviews were carried out at the informant's place of work. Although a questionnaire was used (see appendix B) no attempt was made to restrict the course of the interview to the formal questions. Moreover, in contrast with the situation in the community interviews, the investigator did not refrain from expressing his own views or from commenting on the opinions expressed by the informants. This led in many cases to discussions of the issues that were probably more informative than replies to isolated questions.

In one case three secondary school teachers were interviewed at once and an animated discussion took place, suggesting that this might have been a useful approach if adopted earlier, but this was the last school to be visited. In all other cases the informants were interviewed separately.

Data Collecting and Analysis

The methods used in investigating the attitudes of the teaching sample towards the speech of their pupils were basically the same as those used in investigating the attitudes of the community sample towards Glasgow and the speech of its inhabitants. The information came in the form of response to, and discussion inspired by, open-ended questions. Some of the responses were missing where the structure of an interview made the particular question out of place. The tapes were transcribed in full: all discussions about the teaching sample attitudes is based on these transcriptions and the quotations were taken from them. This material is set out in section 2 of chapter 7.

3. The Employers Sample

The purpose of this sample was to investigate the importance attached to speech by employers, both in the interviewing of job applicants and in considering employees for promotion.

A judgement sample of employers in Glasgow was made in an attempt to cover as wide a range of occupations and levels of employment as possible. The employers include business firms, the Medical Faculty at Glasgow University, the Centre for Secretarial Studies at Strathclyde University, the Corporation Careers Office and an employment agency. The twenty-eight informants were personnel managers, administrators, a Careers Officer and the Director of the employment agency, and the list of informants is given in appendix A.

Interviewing

All the interviews were carried out by the principal investigator. The informants were told that the investigator wanted their opinions on the importance of speech in the interviewing situation and for the purpose of promotion.

None of the informants contacted refused to be interviewed, although four informants refused to have their interview tape-recorded. The interviews were carried out at the informant's place of work. As in the case of the teachers, although a questionnaire was used (see appendix B), no attempt was made to restrict the course of the interview to the formal questions and the investigator did not refrain from expressing his own views or from commenting on the opinions expressed by the informants.

Data Collecting and Analysis

The information came in the form of responses to, and discussion inspired by, open-ended questions. The tapes were transcribed in full: all discussion about the employers sample attitudes is based on these transcriptions and the quotations were taken from them.

4. Linguistic Variation

Owing to the influx of Irish and foreign immigrants in the industrial area near Glasgow the dialect has become hopelessly corrupt.

Grant (1931, xxvii)

THERE IS NO previous account of the language spoken in Glasgow, so it is impossible to approach the description from any historical perspective. Grant and Robson (1926) provide some information about Scottish pronunciation, but it is based mainly on the Lothian varieties. Williams (1912, 9) offers an account of 'that form of Polite Scottish heard from educated speakers in the South-West of Scotland'. Neither of these works provides any direct information about Glasgow speech. McAllister (1963) does give some comments on West of Scotland speech, mainly in the form of strictures about variants to be avoided but she does not go into great detail about the stigmatised forms. It is greatly to be regretted that McAllister has not put in writing the considerable knowledge of Glasgow speech that, as many of her former students recall, she displayed so vividly in her classes at Jordanhill College of Education.

Catford (1957a, 107) classifies Glasgow with Lanarkshire as a nine-vowel system, in his account of 'stressed vowels in monosyllables closed by *t*, i.e. by a voiceless apical stop, which may be either alveolar or dental'. (p.107). The nine vowels (adapted from Catford 1957a, 113) are as follows:

beet	[bit]	*cot*	[kot]
beat ⎫	[bet]	*coat* ⎭	
bait ⎭		*but*	[bʌt]
met	[mɛt]	*about*	[əbʉt]
fat	[fät]	*bit* ⎫	[bët]
faut (= 'fault')	[fɔt]	*boot* ⎭	

None of the informants interviewed in the Glasgow survey used this system consistently, though all forms (with the exception of [bet] for *beat*) were found among a number of speakers.

The inconsistency with which forms are used has led commentators to despair. For example, Winston (1971, 55), dealing with the [ɒ]~[ɔ] distinction, remarks:

> The number of repetitions (of key words), although producing results of some interest, illustrate very convincingly the principle that no one phonetic utterance is reproduced exactly;

25

they serve in the final analysis to confuse rather than clarify the results.

Catford (1957b, 111) attempts to account for this fluctuation in forms by contrasting 'Scots' with 'English':

> A Scotsman may *sound* very Scottish indeed, on account of various phonetic features, but if his phoneme distribution is largely predictable from RP, and if, on the whole, he uses Standard English grammar and lexicon, then we say he is speaking English, although he has a Scottish accent. If, on the other hand, his sound-system differs widely from RP (e.g. including, it may be, additional vowel phonemes, or un-English consonant clusters like [kn-] [wr-] [-xt]), if his phoneme distribution is unpredictable from RP, if his morphology and syntax are un-English (e.g. if he talks about *kye*, has a ternary deictic system, or Scots number-concord, etc.), if he uses words like *callant*, *cuit* and *bide*—then we say he is speaking Scots.

Catford goes on (pp.111–12):

> The classification outlined above provides a framework of terms within which it is useful to operate in discussing Scottish linguistic problems, but, like all such classifications, it is only an approximation. In particular, the distinction between Scots and English is not always so clear-cut or so easy to maintain as might appear. The terms Scots and English refer to two linguistic poles between which there is an almost infinite possibility of dialect mixture. . . . The situation is further complicated by the fact that the majority of habitual Scots speakers are bilingual, in the sense that, though in some social situations they speak a relatively pure Scots, in others they will use an approximation to English, the closeness of the approximation depending both on the nature of the situation itself and on personal characteristics of the speaker (e.g. education, adaptability, conservatism, local patriotism, etc.).

The distinction between Scots and English is certainly not clear-cut nor easy to maintain in Glasgow. There are speakers in the survey interviews who use (though inconsistently) more or less the kind of vowel-system that Catford postulates for Scots; yet, in the interviews, these speakers seldom use dialect words or 'un-English' grammar. It is this kind of situation that is sometimes referred to as 'dialect mixture', but it is far from clear that there are distinct 'dialects' that are mixed. Although the survey does not present any direct evidence on the point, there would appear to be few Glaswegians who habitually speak 'Scots' in the sense that Catford outlines above. What there is in Glasgow is a wide range of pronunciation of 'English'.

26

The situation in Glasgow is very similar to that described by Labov (1966, 6) in New York City:

> We find that in New York City, most idiolects do not form a simple, coherent system: on the contrary, they are studded with oscillations and contradictions both in the organisation of sounds into phonemes, and the organisation of phonemes into larger systems. These inconsistencies are inexplicable in terms of any data within the system. To explain them in terms of borrowing from some other, unknown system is a desperate expedient, which eventually reduces the concept of system to an inconvenient fiction.

The solution that Labov proposed was to examine the linguistic variation for a coherent pattern. By treating the variants for each variable as points along a simple dimension, Labov was able to assign numerical values to each of the variables and average them to produce an index for each variable (Labov 1963, 1966). These indices could then be correlated with extralinguistic variables such as age, sex, social class, and ethnic affiliation. The method employed by Labov in New York City will be applied to the analysis of linguistic variation in Glasgow, with one important difference. Central to Labov's analysis is the notion of stylistic variation as defined for the New York City survey (Labov 1966, chapter IV). As was pointed out in the Introduction (chapter 1), it was not possible to reproduce the sampling of contextual styles in the Glasgow survey, with the result that the axis of stylistic variation is not available for comparison. Despite this limitation, the results from the Glasgow survey show quite clearly that certain features of Glasgow speech co-vary systematically with such factors as age, sex and social class.

Five phonological variables were chosen for detailed analysis on the basis of a preliminary examination of the tapes.[1] They are:

1. (i) the vowel in *hit*, *kill*, *risk*, etc.
2. (u) the vowel in *school*, *book*, *full*, *fool*, etc.
3. (a) the vowel in *hat*, *sad*, *back*, etc.

[1] The original intention was to investigate nine phonological variables. In addition to the five analysed, the original proposal suggested examining the following: (e) e.g. the vowel in *get*, etc.; (ɔ) e.g. the vowel in *off*, etc.; (o) e.g. the vowel in *home*, etc.; (ai) e.g. the diphthong in *side*, etc. The variation in (e) appears to be more a function of intonation than segmental vowel quality. With regard to (ɔ) and (o), where there is clearly variation related to social stratification, the tapes did not provide enough examples of /o/ for (ɔ) or /e/ for (o) to make a quantified analysis feasible. This may have been because of the rather formal tone of the interviews. In the case of (ai) time did not permit a detailed analysis and although all the informants distinguished *tide* /tʌɪd/ from tied /taɪd/ it is not clear at this point whether there is social stratification in the use of this variable.

27

4. (au) the diphthong in *now*, *down*, *house*, etc.

5. (gs) the glottal stop as an alternative to /t/ in *butter*, *get*, etc.

The rationale behind the choice was similar to that given by Labov (1966, 49): 'The most useful items (for intensive study) are those that are high in *frequency*, have a certain *immunity from conscious suppression*, are *integral units of larger structures*, and may be easily *quantified on a linear scale*. By all these criteria, phonological variables appear to be the most useful.'

The second of these criteria, immunity from conscious suppressions, raises problems in Glasgow that are different from those in New York. Many Scots regularly say /hem/, /klez/, /mest/[1] for *home*, *clothes* and *most*, and undoubtedly a number of informants interviewed in the survey would use such forms occasionally or even frequently, yet very few /e/ forms were recorded on the tapes. It seems likely that they were deliberately avoided by the informants. Speitel (1973) refers to such forms as 'primary dialect features' and contrasts them with 'secondary dialect features', which he claims are less under conscious control. However, Speitel also includes pronunciations such as /hus/, /əbut/ and /dun/ for *house*, *about* and *down* as primary dialect features, and examples of these pronunciations are quite common on the Glasgow interview tapes. The reason for the difference between the two features is that the pronunciation /u/ is the highest point on a continuous dimension from /au/ with a range of intervening stages, whereas /e/ and /o/ are alternatives without intermediate variants. As a result there may be a very small articulatory difference between a centralised variety of /au/ and /u/ but there will always be a much greater articulatory difference between /e/ and /o/. Consequently, in the latter case the speaker must deliberately choose to say either /hem/ or /hom/. Moreover, it is only in a relatively small number of words that /e/ may occur for /o/, whereas there is less restriction on /u/ for /au/. Accordingly, variables such as (au) are suitable for detailed study both because they are easily quantified and because they are relatively immune to conscious suppression. The situation is exactly the opposite with the alternation between /o/ and /e/, and the latter will not be dealt with in detail here.

Romaine (1975), however, points out that the two extreme points

[1] The use of symbols in this book follows that of previous investigators. Parentheses are used to represent variables, e.g. (au), slashes to indicate a broad phonetic transcription without assumptions as to the phonological status of the segment, e.g. /u/, and square brackets to indicate a narrower phonetic transcription, e.g. [ï˙]. Thus, for example, a reference to /æ/ and /a/ as variants of (a) is not intended to indicate that there is a phonemic contrast between /æ/ and /a/ but rather that the precise phonetic quality of the front or back variant is not of interest for the point being made.

of the (au) continuum can be the subject of deliberate choice as much as the alternation between /e/ and /o/, and she quotes a ten-year-old girl in Edinburgh whose mother sometimes corrected her pronunciation of *down* from /dun/ to /daun/. Romaine asked the girl if her teacher ever said anything to her about the way she spoke. 'I've never actually said /dun/ to the teacher', replied the girl. This shows a clear awareness of the choice available in the use of this variable and Romaine is right to draw attention to it. Nevertheless, Romaine's decision to treat (au) as a discrete variable alternating between /u/ and /au/ risks losing some information. Many Glaswegians who seldom or never realise (au) as monophthongal /u/ will occasionally use a very centralised diphthong with only a very brief on-glide. To treat this realisation as equivalent either to /u/ or some much less centralised variety of /au/ seems arbitrary. As will be seen, below, when (au) is treated as a continuous variable something approaching a normal curve of distribution is found. Thus, although Romaine is right to draw attention to the perceptual dichotomy between /u/ and /au/ for this variable, the fact that intermediate variants also occur justifies treating it differently from the /e/~/o/ alternation.

A more serious criticism has been raised by Aitken (personal communication). Aitken points out that in two of the variables, (u) and (au), there are confounding factors because the tokens that were extracted and analysed for each variable may not come from lexical items belonging to the same word class. This problem was anticipated with regard to the variable (a). In extracting tokens of (a) care was taken to select only those examples that belong to the /æ/ class in RP and to avoid those belonging to the /ɑː/ class in RP. The reason for this was uncertainty as to the extent to which the /æ/~/ɑː/ distinction would be found in Glasgow. Although only three speakers (all belonging to class I) made a distinction between *Sam* and *psalm* in reading the list of minimal pairs, several other speakers used a low back vowel in words that belong to the RP /ɑː/ class. Some of these speakers also used a back vowel in lexical items belonging to the RP /æ/ class. For such speakers there appeared to be nothing that corresponds to the /æ/~/ɑː/ distinction in RP. It was unclear, however, from those speakers who usually used a front vowel for words in the RP /æ/ class and occasionally a back vowel in words from the RP /ɑː/ class, whether they had a consistent distinction and, if so, which lexical items belonged in each word class. This is obviously a question that deserves further investigation, but the data from the present survey are insufficient to provide an answer. It was for this reason that the analysis of the (a) variable was limited to those items that belong to the RP /æ/ class, even though the RP distinction is probably irrelevant for most of the speakers in the sample.

In the case of (u) there is a much more serious danger of confusion, which was not taken into account at the time of analysis. The tokens extracted for analysis were taken from those lexical items that belong to the RP /uː/ and /ʊ/ classes. Aitken points out that only some of these, e.g. *boot*, *school*, etc., will have unrounded front variants in the neighbourhood of [ɪ]; others, e.g. *pull*, *push*, etc., have unrounded back variants in the region of [ʌ]. Still other lexical items, e.g. *shoe*, *lose*, etc., will never have unrounded variants. In the form of analysis adopted here no attempt was made to keep these words classes distinct, implying that an unrounded variant (coded u–4) was equally possible for all lexical items. Because of the form in which the examples were extracted and coded it is not easy at this stage to ascertain what effect this error may have caused, and the best that can be hoped is that the distortion is relatively slight. The number of tokens coded (u–4) was 285, or approximately sixteen per cent of the total for all informants. If these items had been omitted from the calculations the same pattern of social stratification would have been revealed, although the distance between the social class groups would be less pronounced. Because of the problems of re-analysis at this stage it was decided to let the original analysis stand, with the warning that it may give a distorted picture of the situation because the variable is more complex than had been realised.

In the case of (au) there are a number of Scots words, e.g. *coup*, *howff*, that never occur with a monophthongal variant. If a large number of these lexical items had occurred in the data there would have been a risk of confusion similar to that which arose in the case of the (u) variable. However, the only lexical item of this kind to occur in the whole corpus was *coup*, and since all the respondents used it in answer to a question about its meaning the risk of distortion through its inclusion is very slight. With this exception only lexical items from the RP /au/ class were analysed.[1]

The notion of 'word class' is an important one and deserves more thorough investigation. However, it probably cannot be done simply by analysing samples of speech in the interview situation alone. Instead, both the speaker's judgements and samples of his speech in less formal situations will be necessary.

The Variable (i)

This is the vowel in *hit*, *fill*, *pin*, etc., and variation in the quality of the vowel in Scottish English is noted by Grant and Robson (1926). They give six variants, in addition to the SSE form (p.86): [ε¹, ε-,

---

[1] The two instances of [aʊər] and [sʌʊl] were not treated as examples of (au).

30

ə⊥, ʌ, ᶩ, ï]. McAllister (1963, 140–1) gives three variants: [ᶩ], 'a vowel produced with the tongue slightly lower than the position for [i]'; [ɪ-], 'a form of [ɪ] made with the tongue slightly farther back than it is for [i]'; and [ɪ⁾], 'another very frequent Clydeside variant, produced by giving the vowel half-rounding. The lower lip is protruded slightly forward.' She adds (p.141): 'Speakers of local dialect will find it most difficult to maintain the vowel at its brightest pitch when it comes immediately before or after [l, m, n, ŋ, s].'

In the present survey all these variants were noted with the exception of [ɪ⁾], which did not emerge as an identifiable variant on the tapes. The variants were codified on a five-point scale as follows:

(i–1)   [ɪ]
(i–2)   [ε^] and [ɪᵥ]
(i–3)   [ε>] and [ïᵥ]
(i–4)   [ə^]
(i–5)   [ʌ^]

For each informant forty instances of (i) from the first half of the tape and forty instances from the second half of the tape were extracted and assigned values from one to five.[1] The values for each informant were then averaged and multiplied by 100, giving an index figure between 100 and 500. The two halves of the tape were analysed separately in case there was a stylistic shift in the course of the interview. Table 1 shows a slight upward shift for almost all groups: for all informants the average index for the first forty tokens is 251 and for the second forty tokens 262. There was then, in general, a tendency for the index to rise as the interview proceeded. This would be expected if the rise indicates a movement towards more informal speech, but the difference is seldom considerable.

More interesting is the distribution through social class, sex and age. Table 2 gives the figures for the four classes as a whole, and shows that the mean indices for (i) increase from the highest social class group to the lowest. In articulatory terms this indicates that the speakers from the lower social class groups are more likely to use a vowel that is more retracted and lowered than speakers from the higher social class groups. There is also a clear indication of sex

[1] Only tokens of (i) in fully-stressed syllables were extracted and instances before /r/ were omitted since they require separate investigation. To avoid bias from frequently used words, no more than three tokens of a single lexical item were extracted. These restrictions apply to the variables (u), (au) and (a) as well. Some speakers used fewer than the maximum number of tokens to be extracted; in such cases all the tokens used by the speaker were extracted, subject to the previously mentioned restrictions.

differences; in each social class group the mean indices of females are lower than those for males. Moreover, there is an interesting interaction between social class and sex in that the greatest difference between the mean indices for males comes between class ɪ and class ɪɪa, whereas for females it comes between class ɪɪa and class ɪɪb. In other words, class ɪɪa females are fairly similar to class ɪ females in their use of (i), but class ɪɪa males are closer to class ɪɪb males than they are to class ɪ males. The difference between the social class groups is smallest between class ɪɪb and class ɪɪɪ. Since a similar pattern is found in the other variables there are grounds for suggesting, as will be argued in chapter 5, that classes ɪɪb and ɪɪɪ should be grouped together into a single class. This does not mean that there are no systematic differences between these groups, but they are much smaller than those between the other groups. However, the results for all four social class groups will be presented separately to show the extent of these differences. (See chapter 5 and Macaulay 1976 for further discussion of social class in Glasgow.)

Table 1. Indices for the variable (i) by age and class: first 40 tokens *vs* second 40 tokens

	Adults		15-yr-olds		10-yr-olds	
	1st 40	2nd 40	1st 40	2nd 40	1st 40	2nd 40
Class ɪ	168	180	200	198	230	240
Class ɪɪa	238	238	244	254	255	266
Class ɪɪb	286	288	280	308	263	277
Class ɪɪɪ	280	286	299	313	288	299

An interesting effect of age can be seen in table 3, which shows that the mean indices for fifteen-year-olds are generally higher than those for adults in the same social class group, and in classes ɪ and ɪɪa the mean indices for ten-year-olds are higher than those for fifteen-year-olds. This pattern is clearest among the class ɪ ten-year-olds, who are closer to their peers in the other social class groups than are the adults or the fifteen-year-olds. In other words, the distance between the social class groups increases with age.

Table 2. Indices for the variable (i) by social class

	ɪ	ɪɪa	ɪɪb	ɪɪɪ	All
All	202	247	284	294	257
Males	224	279	287	300	273
Females	180	215	280	288	242

There is also an interesting sex difference in that class I fifteen-year-old girls are much closer to class I women in their use of this variable than class I fifteen-year-old boys are to class I men. This may either reflect a greater awareness of the social significance of the variable among the girls, or indicate that for the class I boys working-class speech holds the kind of favourable connotations Trudgill (1972) found among male speakers in Norwich. The one anomaly in table 3 is the mean index for class II b ten-year-old boys, which is lower than the mean indices for the fifteen-year-olds and adults in the same social class, and the lowest index of the ten-year-old boys. There is no obvious explanation for this unexpected result.

Table 3. Indices for the variable (i)
by age, sex, and social class

	I	IIa	IIb	III
Adults	174	238	287	283
15-yr-olds	199	249	294	308
10-yr-olds	235	261	270	291
Men	189	269	305	301
15-yr-old boys	234	279	308	296
10-yr-old boys	250	290	248	302
Women	158	206	269	264
15-yr-old girls	163	219	279	319
10-yr-old girls	220	231	291	280

The first forty tokens from each informant were also analysed in terms of the phonetic contexts in which each occurred. The preceding and following phonetic environments for each token were tabulated and the values of (i) in that context averaged.

Table 4 shows that for all informants higher values of (i) are recorded in the environment of voiced consonants than in the environment of voiceless consonants. It can also be seen that there is no difference between the effect of a preceding voiceless consonant and that of a following voiceless consonant, but in the case of voiced consonants a following voiced consonant is likely to produce slightly higher values of (i), although the difference is not nearly as great as the difference between voiced and voiceless consonants.

The effect of nasal and lateral consonants was also investigated. Table 5 shows their effects, contrasted with those of all consonants (i.e. including nasals and laterals). It can be seen that laterals have the greatest effect, producing much higher values of (i) whether they precede or follow the vowel. With nasals there is a

Table 4. Indices for the first 40 instances of the variable (i) in phonetic context: distribution by age and class, showing the effect of voiced and voiceless consonants

	Adults				15-yr-olds				10-yr-olds				All age groups				All
	I	IIa	IIb	III	I	IIa	IIb	III	I	IIa	IIb	III	I	IIa	IIb	III	
Voiceless Preceding	147	227	265	270	194	224	265	297	225	246	258	279	189	232	263	282	242
Voiceless Following	154	217	268	274	190	226	265	283	230	245	243	292	191	229	259	283	241
Voiced Preceding	179	244	313	301	223	265	310	324	259	268	302	318	220	259	308	314	275
Voiced Following	184	270	315	332	253	296	335	334	273	297	312	322	233	288	321	329	293

Table 5. Indices for the first 40 instances of the variable (i) in phonetic context: distribution by age and class, showing the effect of nasal and lateral consonants

	Adults				15-yr-olds				10-yr-olds				All age groups				All
	I	IIa	IIb	III	I	IIa	IIb	III	I	IIa	IIb	III	I	IIa	IIb	III	
Nasals Preceding	174	233	287	318	200	292	304	344	250	300	225	300	208	275	272	321	269
Nasals Following	143	217	259	250	165	219	249	271	208	226	235	255	172	221	248	259	225
Laterals Preceding	216	285	336	360	280	287	373	383	244	315	360	387	247	296	356	377	319
Laterals Following	180	325	375	367	271	375	360	400	216	350	365	325	222	350	367	364	326
All Consonants Preceding	159	239	288	297	236	257	280	324	159	239	288	297	185	245	285	306	255
All Consonants Following	160	226	279	283	197	229	279	291	160	226	279	285	172	227	279	286	241

Table 6. Indices for the first 40 instances of the variable (i) in phonetic context: distribution by age and class, showing the effect of place of articulation of preceding or following consonant

	Adults				15-yr-olds				10-yr-olds				All age groups				All	Combined contexts
	I	IIa	IIb	III	I	IIa	IIb	III	I	IIa	IIb	III	I	IIa	IIb	III		
Bilabials Preceding	148	241	303	296	213	273	283	319	256	273	262	307	208	262	283	307	265	260
Bilabials Following	172	237	302	250	188	200	283	271	275	290	283	275	218	242	289	265	254	
Labio-dentals Preceding	168	219	273	258	212	253	288	308	210	281	270	290	197	251	277	285	253	260
Labio-dentals Following	180	231	293	330	208	259	292	296	271	269	306	271	220	253	297	299	267	
/θ/ Preceding	146	207	235	239	175	216	233	251	225	248	235	244	182	224	234	245	221	
Alveolars Preceding	155	232	250	256	195	226	274	291	217	237	255	279	189	232	260	275	239	243
Alveolars Following	158	224	274	278	182	224	270	296	235	269	246	310	192	239	263	295	247	
Alveo-palatals Preceding	200	261	329	366	300	300	—	350	275	254	267	275	258	272	298	330	290	271
Alveo-palatals Following	162	224	272	293	233	250	300	316	225	278	250	217	207	251	274	275	252	
Velars Preceding	125	241	283	310	258	233	275	350	243	256	274	278	209	243	277	313	261	244
Velars Following	130	212	252	262	175	212	252	275	218	225	237	264	174	216	247	267	226	
/h/ Preceding	200	250	366	300	233	266	303	300	200	300	283	275	211	272	317	325	281	

marked contrast between a preceding nasal, which produces higher than normal values of (i), and a following nasal, which produces lower than normal values of (i). The reason for this contrast is probably due to the influence of velar nasals, which only occur in the following environment. As will be shown below, a following velar consonant generally occurs with relatively low values of (i).

Table 6, which gives the results of the analysis of phonetic environment by place of articulation, shows that bilabials and labiodentals are associated with slightly higher values of (i) than are alveolars and velars, taking the averages for the combined contexts. This would make sense in articulatory terms since the raising of the tongue towards the palate for alveolars and velars could produce a higher level quality. However, there are several problems with this interpretation. The first is the high values of (i) associated with alveo-palatals, particularly preceding alveo-palatals. The second is the difference between a preceding velar consonant and a following one. Preceding velars are associated with a high value of (i), 261 for all informants, while following velars are found with a very low value of (i), 226 for all informants. It is obvious that a combination of preceding and following consonants must affect the quality of the vowel. For example, the lowest values of (i) are found with preceding /θ/. The next lowest values of (i) are found with a following velar consonant. It is also shown in table 5 that a following nasal consonant is associated with low values of (i). The combination of these three factors is found in the words *thing* and *think*, which form the bulk of the examples with preceding /θ/, though in fact the total number of examples is not large.

It is probably not a coincidence that low values of (i) are found with all three phonetic conditions.[1] Another example is the word *children*, which is one of the most common examples of a preceding alveo-palatal. As shown in table 5 laterals are associated with high values of (i), so that the figures for preceding alveo-palatals may be effected by the large number of instances of the word *children* in the data. Unfortunately, the effect of combined environments cannot be easily calculated from the figures at present available and the exploration of this point will have to be left to a later date. However, a tentative ranking of the effect of place of articulation can be given on the basis of the figures in table 6:

	high ↑	preceding /h/ and alveo-palatals
values		bilabials and labio-dentals
of (i)		alveolars and velars
	low	preceding /θ/

[1] In a sample of twelve speakers, eleven showed lower values of (i) in the context /θ___ŋ/ than in the rest of the interview. The average value

What is particularly impressive about the figures in table 6 is the general consistency across age and social class groups. Thus, for example, although the highest value for class ı adults (200) is lower than the lowest value for class ııı adults (239), the general pattern of effect of place of articulation is maintained, with minor discrepancies. This shows that the phonetic factors affecting the quality of (i) are common to all members of the speech community and that the differences among the groups must be due to non-phonetic factors.

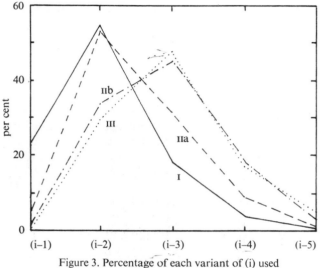

Figure 3. Percentage of each variant of (i) used
by the four social class groups (adults only)

In fact, each social class group seems to have its favoured variant or target. Figure 3 shows the percentage of each variant for the four social classes (adults only), and it can be seen that the locus for the two lower social class groups is (i–3) whereas for the two higher social class groups it is (i–2); only class ı adults used (i–1) with any frequency. The number of tokens of each variant used by a speaker and its relative frequency are given in appendix c (tables 1–3). These figures give some reassurance that a great deal of variance is not being concealed by the use of indices representing the average value of all the tokens tabulated. However, inevitably some information is lost. For example, speaker 010, with an index of 267, used 38% (i–2), 57% (i–3) and 5% (i–4) while speaker 055, with an index of 268, used 2.5% (i–1), 45% (i–2), 37.5% (i–3),

of (i) in the context /θ____ŋ/ for the twelve speakers was 250 compared with an overall mean index of 280 for (i) for these same speakers.

37

12.5% (i–4) and 2.5% (i–5). Thus the almost identical indices conceal rather different uses of the variable. It is for this reason that Berdan (1976) has argued that the use of variant counts is a more reliable measure than the use of indices. On the other hand there are relatively few cases like this, and even in this case the differences between the speakers is not large. Secondly, the number of tokens available for tabulation from speakers 010 and 055 was only half that normally extracted; a longer sample of speech might have reduced the discrepancy. Thirdly, it is significant that there are no bimodal distributions for individuals for any of the variables. In other words, it is never the case that a speaker uses two non-contiguous variants more frequently than an intervening variant. On the whole, the decision to treat the vowel variables as continuous rather than discrete variables seems justified by the results.

The use of the variable (i) reveals some important aspects of linguistic variation in Glasgow. First of all, there is clear evidence of social stratification in the use of the variable, though the differences between classes IIb and III are relatively small. Secondly, there are differences related to sex, with females, particularly in class IIa, tending to use more prestige variants and fewer stigmatised variants. Thirdly, social class differences are greater among the adults than among the ten-year-olds, which suggests that the prestige variants are acquired by classes I and IIa during adolescence. Fourthly, the fact that in classes I and IIa the fifteen-year-old girls are closer to the adults in their use of this variable than are the fifteen-year-old boys suggests either that the girls are more aware of the social significance of this variable or that the boys are more resistant to social pressures to conform to the adult standards of their social class group. Finally, phonetic context appears to affect the quality of the vowel for all speakers approximately to the same degree.

The Variable (u)

This is the vowel in *school*, *book*, *full*, *fool*, etc., since there is no contrast in most forms of Scottish English between *fool* /fuːl/ and *full* /ful/. McAllister (1963, 161) says that 'it is made with the tongue advanced towards the position for central vowels and with a much closer and tenser lip rounding than the standard vowel. . . . The local pronunciation of /u/ (*do*) is produced with the lips closely rounded against the teeth, the centre of the upper lip being drawn downwards to the lower lip.' She also mentions one local variant: 'A Clydeside variant of this vowel is produced with the tongue advanced but with only half-rounding.'

In the survey tapes four varieties of (u) were noted and codified on a four-point scale as follows:

(u–1) [ᶜu]
(u–2) [ü]
(u–3) [ʉ]
(u–4) [ɪᵛ] or [ɪʊ]

For each speaker all the instances of (u) were extracted and assigned the appropriate values.[1] The values for each informant were then averaged and multiplied by 100, giving an index figure between 100 and 400.

Table 7 shows that, as in the case of the variable (i), there is clear social stratification in the use of the variable (u), though the results must be interpreted more cautiously because of the uncertainty caused by the conflation of different word classes. In articulatory terms, the increase in the mean indices from class I to class III indicates that speakers from the two lower social class groups are more likely to use an extremely fronted (and sometimes unrounded) variant of (u) than are the speakers in classes I and IIa. The range of variants for the adult speakers is shown in figure 4, where it can be seen that only the class I adults used a substantial proportion of (u–1) while only class IIb and class III speakers used (u–4) to any considerable extent. The number of tokens of each variant used by a speaker and its relative frequency are given in appendix C (tables 4–6).

Table 7. Indices for the variable (u) by social class

	I	IIa	IIb	III	All
All	178	234	295	312	256
Males	193	241	305	308	262
Females	164	228	287	317	249

Table 8 shows the indices distributed by age and sex. In all social class groups except class III the mean indices for adults are lower than those for both groups of younger speakers. In class III the reverse is true, but in that social class group all three age-groups show very high values for (u). As was the case with the variable (i), in classes I and IIa the fifteen-year-old girls are closer to the adults in their use of the variable (u) than are the fifteen-year-old boys. Thus the use of the variable (u) confirms the pattern of linguistic variation revealed in the use of the variable (i).

[1] As pointed out above (p.30) there are serious problems with this coding system because it conflates several word classes. The two instances of [ʌ] for (u) were coded (u–4).

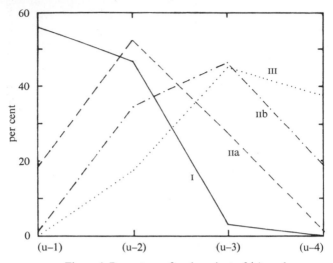

Figure 4. Percentage of each variant of (u) used
by the four social class groups (adults only)

Table 8. Indices for the variable (u)
by age, sex, and social class

	I	IIa	IIb	III
Adults	145	212	284	321
15-yr-olds	192	237	298	314
10-yr-olds	200	261	306	304
Men	157	224	298	323
15-yr-old boys	223	256	312	296
10-yr-old boys	199	254	304	305
Women	132	199	269	318
15-yr-old girls	160	217	283	331
10-yr-old girls	201	268	308	303

The Variable (au)

This is the diphthong in *now*, *down*, *house*, etc. According to
McAllister (1963, 179–80): 'Scottish /au/ is narrower than Southern
English /ɑ‹ʊ/ because of the difference in quality between "front a"
and "back a".' She adds that 'local tendencies to use tense vowels
for the diphthong lead to a modification of /ɑ‹ʊ/, the tense /ʌu/
being substituted for it.' Williams (1912, 53) does not mention the
possibility of a centralised vowel for (au). She merely comments

40

that 'the chief difference in Scotland is the substitution of /u/ for the English /ʊ/.'

In the survey tapes four varieties of (au) were isolated and codified on a four-point scale as follows:

(au–1) [ɑˇʊ]
(au–2) [ʌu]
(au–3) [əu]
(au–4) [ˇu], [ü] or [ʉ]

For each speaker all the instances of (au) were extracted and assigned the appropriate values. When averaged and multiplied by 100 this produced index figures between 100 and 400. The distribution according to social class, age and sex, is given in tables 9 and 10.

Table 9. Indices for the variable (au) by social class

	I	IIa	IIb	III	All
All	212	268	335	348	291
Males	229	279	332	356	299
Females	196	257	337	341	283

Table 10. Indices for the variable (au) by age, sex and social class

	I	IIa	IIb	III
Adults	152	247	334	362
15-yr-olds	242	286	349	342
10-yr-olds	244	272	322	343
Men	186	271	338	358
15-yr-old boys	263	287	348	351
10-yr-old boys	239	278	310	359
Women	117	222	330	365
15-yr-old girls	221	285	349	332
10-yr-old girls	249	266	333	326

Once again the pattern of social stratification found in the (i) and (u) variables appears, and again there is a slight tendency for the mean indices of males to be higher than those of females. However, as table 10 shows, perhaps the most striking aspect of this variable is the difference in class I between the mean indices of adults and those of both groups of children. In particular, class I and class IIa fifteen-year-old girls show relatively high values of (au). Figure 5 shows the percentage of variants used by the adult speakers, and it can be seen that class I adults mainly used (au–1) and (au–2), class

41

iia adults mostly used (au–2) and (au–3), whereas the adults in classes iib and iii used (au–3) and (au–4) most frequently. The numbers and percentages of each variant used by a speaker are given in appendix c (tables 7–9). It is only class i adults who used (au–1) frequently, and among the class i and class iia speakers only the class iia fifteen-year-olds used (au–4) regularly.

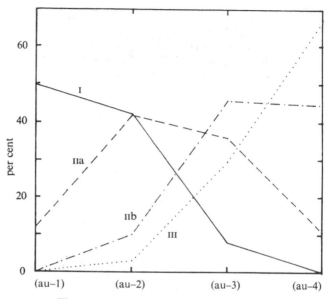

Figure 5. Percentage of each variant of (au) used
by the four social class groups (adults only)

The Variable (a)

This is the vowel in *cap*, *bag*, etc., and it presents particular problems for analysis because the range of variation is less than for the other vowel variables.[1] There is no contrast for most of the informants between the minimal pair in Received Pronunciation of *Sam* [sæm] and *psalm* [sɑːm]. The usual vowel for words of both types is a low central vowel, which may be advanced or retracted.

However, it is not true that Glasgow speakers never use /ɑː/. The problem arises because it may be used in different ways by different speakers. Some speakers who use /æ/ in *cap*, *bag*, etc., will

[1] In the original analysis (see Macaulay and Trevelyan 1973, 58-60), the variable (a), contrary to expectation, did not show consistent correlation with social class. When the data were re-analysed using a slightly different coding scheme the expected pattern emerged.

42

use /ɑ:/ in *father, Glasgow*, and *after* but not usually in *dance, path, psalm*, or *class*, so that there is a contrast similar to that found in RP but with a different distribution. Other speakers who use /ɑ:/ in *father, Glasgow*, etc., may also use the same sound in *bag, hand*, etc., so that no contrast of the kind found in RP occurs; although there may be considerable variation in the vowel quality it does not correspond to any division according to word classes. This variation goes back at least sixty years. Williams (1912) observes: 'Some Scottish speakers use the same sound in all these words, *path, father, hat*, some pronounce the *a* in *hard* differently to the other three, others *hard* and *father* alike, and *path* and *hat*.' Later she comments: 'The use of /ɑ:/ for all the words under discussion is sometimes heard but should be avoided. . . . I have heard the /ɑ:/ more frequently from men than from women.'

McAllister (1963, 153) also mentions that 'those who use a local dialect . . . make no distinction between the *a* in *are* and the *a* in *fat*, using "back a" for both.' She later warns (p.153): 'In acquiring "front a", care should be taken not to raise the front of the tongue to the position for /ɛ/. The use of "back a" for "front a" is preferable to this', and she adds (p.155): 'Those acquiring "front a" will find it necessary to concentrate upon its use, particularly before and after the plosives /k/ and /g/ and the nasals /m, n, ŋ/.'

Accordingly, for the present analysis all words that belong in the /ɑ:/ class in RP are excluded and the variable (a) is restricted to words that would have /æ/ in RP. The variants were codified on a three-point scale as follows:

(a–1)   [æ] or [ˠa]
(a–2)   [a]
(a–3)   [aˠ], [ˠɑ], [ɑ] or [ɒ]

For each informant forty instances of (a) were extracted and assigned the appropriate values. The values for each informant were then averaged and multiplied by 100, giving an index figure between 100 and 300. The distribution according to social class, age, and sex is given in tables 11 and 12.

Table 11 shows that there is clear social stratification in the use of the (a) variable, with the lower social class groups using a more retracted vowel and only the class I speakers and the class IIa

Table 11. Indices for the variable (a) by social class

	I	IIa	IIb	III	All
All	158	190	242	253	211
Males	165	208	243	254	218
Females	150	171	241	252	205

females using a front vowel. Table 12 shows that sex and age differences are less clearly marked than in the case of the other variables. It is only in class I that the adults consistently show lower values of (a) than the younger speakers, and it is only among class I and class IIa adults and fifteen-year-olds that there are clear sex differences.

Table 12. Indices for the variable (a)
by age, sex, and social class

	I	IIa	IIb	III
Adults	133	201	261	260
15-yr-olds	165	200	234	264
10-yr-olds	176	169	247	236
Men	143	228	264	263
15-yr-old boys	182	223	237	261
10-yr-old boys	171	173	228	238
Women	123	174	257	257
15-yr-old girls	148	176	230	266
10-yr-old girls	180	164	237	233

Figure 6 shows the percentage of each variant used by the adult speakers. The most frequent variant for class I is (a–1), for class IIa (a–2), and for classes IIb and III it is (a–3). The number and percentage of each variant used by a speaker are given in appendix c (tables 10–12). It turns out that most speakers alternated between (a–1) and (a–2), or between (a–2) and (a–3); there were very few speakers who used all three variants.

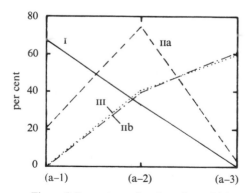

Figure 6. Percentage of each variant of (a) used
by the four social class groups (adults only)

Glottal Stops

Of all features of Glasgow speech the most notorious is the glottal stop, and it was the feature most frequently singled out by teachers as characteristic of a Glasgow accent (see chapter 8). In order to investigate the incidence of this feature, forty tokens of post-tonic potential /t/ were extracted from the first half of the tape and forty tokens from the second half of the tape. By post-tonic is meant following the main stress, so that, for example, in the word *paternity* the first /t/ is not a possible context for a glottal stop but the second /t/ is. Each occurrence of a glottal stop was given the value 1 and each occurrence of /t/ the value 0. When averaged and multiplied by 100 this produced a percentage index for glottal stops ranging from 0 for those who used no glottal stops to 100 for those who used only glottal stops in this context. Since there were few systematic differences between the first forty and the second forty tokens, the average of the eighty tokens was taken as the index for this variable.

Table 13. Percentage indices for (gs) by social class

	I	IIa	IIb	III	All
All	48.4	72.9	84.3	91.7	74.3
Males	48.5	80.8	84.0	93.5	76.7
Females	48.3	64.4	84.7	90.0	71.9

It can be seen from table 13 that the use of glottal stops is indeed extensive in Glasgow. There is clear social stratification but sex differences are much less clearly marked, except in class IIa, where females used almost twenty per cent fewer glottal stops than males. The details can be seen in table 14, where perhaps the most surprising feature is the relatively high percentage of glottal stops used by class I girls, higher in fact than the class I boys. On the other hand, in class IIa it was the boys who used a very high percentage of glottal stops.

However, the percentages in tables 13 and 14 do not take into consideration the following phonetic context. To investigate this the percentage of glottal stops occurring a) before a pause, b) before a vowel, and c) before a consonant was calculated.

Figure 7 shows that the differences between the social class groups are much greater before a pause or a vowel than before a consonant. To demonstrate this, the indices were re-calculated omitting the tokens before a consonant, and these percentages are given in table 15, which reveals an even clearer pattern of social

Table 14. Percentage indices for (gs)
by age, sex, and social class

	I	IIa	IIb	III
Adults	35.9	54.4	84.4	91.6
15-yr-olds	43.5	78.3	84.3	95.6
10-yr-olds	66.0	85.7	84.4	88.2
Men	38.7	60.0	87.5	93.1
15-yr-old boys	41.9	93.1	86.9	95.5
10-yr-old boys	65.0	89.4	77.5	91.9
Women	33.1	48.8	81.2	90.0
15-yr-old girls	45.0	63.5	81.7	95.6
10-yr-old girls	66.9	81.9	91.2	84.4

Table 15. Percentage indices for (gs) before a pause
and before a vowel, by social class

	I	IIa	IIb	III	All
All	30.9	60.2	79.7	90.4	65.3
Males	30.9	74.7	80.0	93.6	69.8
Females	30.9	45.6	79.4	87.1	60.8

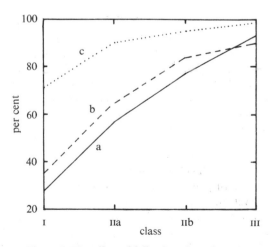

Figure 7. The effect of following phonetic context
on the variable (gs): (a) before a pause, (b) before
a vowel, and (c) before a consonant

stratification than table 13 did. It also brings out more clearly the sex differences, with class IIa females using forty per cent fewer glottal stops than class IIa males. A possible explanation for this is that the use of glottal stops is the most openly stigmatised feature of Glasgow speech (see chapter 8) and thus may be more consciously avoided by those who are concerned about the correctness of their speech. One of the class IIa female speakers used no glottal stops before a vowel or a pause. This is fewer than any of the class I speakers and fits the notion of hypercorrection suggested by Labov (1966b).

Table 16. Percentage indices for (gs) before a pause and before a vowel, by age, sex, and social class

	I	IIa	IIb	III
Adults	10.3	27.1	77.8	90.2
15-yr-olds	14.9	69.2	79.8	94.9
10-yr-olds	57.5	84.3	81.8	86.0
Men	11.3	41.6	89.1	92.3
15-yr-old boys	25.0	92.6	81.7	95.6
10-yr-old boys	56.2	89.9	69.4	92.8
Women	9.3	12.5	66.4	88.0
15-yr-old girls	24.8	45.7	77.8	94.1
10-yr-old girls	58.7	78.7	94.1	79.2

Table 16 brings out the effects of sex and age more clearly. In class I there is virtually no difference between males and females but there are considerable differences between the age groups, with the ten-year-olds using almost six times as many glottal stops as the adults. Class IIa shows the largest sex differences, with males using a much higher percentage of glottal stops than females; there are also substantial age differences in this class, with the fifteen-year-old boys showing a particularly high percentage of glottal stops. In class IIb the mean indices for the ten-year-old boys are much lower than for the ten-year-old girls; this is similar to the pattern displayed in the use of the variable (i), but once again there is no obvious explanation. In class III there are only very slight age and sex differences with all speakers using a very high percentage of glottal stops, the lowest being the ten-year-old girls with 79.2%.

Appendix C (tables 13–15) gives the percentage of glottal stops for each informant in the three environments: before a consonant, before a vowel, and before a pause. It is clear that the class I and IIa adults and the class I fifteen-year-olds were less likely to use a glottal stop before a pause than before a vowel. However, as Romaine (1975) points out, the environment before a vowel includes three contexts, which may have different effects: a) word medial with no morphemic boundary, e.g. *water*; b) word medial before a morphemic boundary, e.g. *started*; and c) word final before a vowel in the following word, e.g. *that* (*is*). There were too few examples of a) and b) to allow a breakdown into these three categories, but if a) and b) are grouped together in contrast to c) an interesting difference between word medial position and word final position appears.

Table 17. The effect of word boundary on glottal stops
before a vowel (adults only)

	I	IIa	IIb	III
Word medial	0.0	7.2	42.5	68.8
Word final	25.0	49.3	89.0	91.8

Table 17 shows the percentage of glottal stops used in these two categories. It can be seen that glottal stops are much more likely to occur in word final position before a vowel in the following word than they are in word medial position. In fact, among the class I adults glottal stops are categorically absent from word medial position, although they occur with a frequency of 25% in word final position before a following vowel. There is also a social class difference, in that the ratio of glottal stops in word medial position to their occurrence in word final position before a following vowel is 1:7 in class IIa, 1:2 in class IIb and 3:4 in class III. This shows that Romaine is correct in her suggestion that the word medial environment is likely to be more highly stigmatised.

Religious Differences

It has been shown that there are systematic differences in the use of the variables (i), (u), (au), (a) and (gs) that correlate with age, sex, and social class. The remaining extra-linguistic variable to be considered is religion. Exactly one quarter of the sample were Catholics and thus it is possible to compare them with the remainder of the informants. The figures for the five variables are given in table 18, which shows that while there are numerous differences between Catholics and non-Catholics, there is no overall pattern to these differences. The only consistent difference between the two groups is that Catholic fifteen-year-olds are much closer to their parents in the use of the variables (i), (u), and (au) than is the case with the non-Catholic group. This might indicate closer family ties among the Catholics, but it is not true of the ten-year-olds, nor of the (gs) variable, and it would be mere speculation to attempt to explain these differences. On the basis of the five variables analysed there

48

would seem to be little evidence that religion is a significant factor in linguistic variation in Glasgow.

Table 18. Indices for all five variables
by age, class, and religion

(i)	Adults	15-yr-olds	10-yr-olds	I	IIa	IIb	III
Catholics	260	253	224	187	247	243	292
Non-Catholics	239	264	276	207	248	290	294
(u)							
Catholics	237	246	275	170	272	305	293
Non-Catholics	241	264	263	181	229	294	322
(au)							
Catholics	283	293	307	231	296	315	349
Non-Catholics	269	308	291	206	267	338	348
(a)							
Catholics	226	217	191	155	204	236	247
Non-Catholics	209	215	207	159	185	243	256
(gs)							
Catholics	50	73	67	33	77	52	88
Non-Catholics	52	65	80	32	46	82	91

Intonation

As Crystal (1971b) points out, prosodic and paralinguistic features have generally been ignored in sociolinguistic work. It is easy to understand why. Such features are hard to describe and even harder to quantify. Even in describing the intonation of Standard English there is no single accepted system of notation so that comparisons are difficult. This is particularly unfortunate, because probably the most immediately noticeable features of a stranger's speech are prosodic and paralinguistic, and thus they may provide important clues for sociolinguistic identification.

In the Glasgow survey, time did not permit a full investigation of prosodic or paralinguistic features, but it was decided to make an exploratory investigation of intonation. Two tapes were selected, the first ten minutes of each transcribed and the intonation patterns analysed. The two speakers chosen were 045, a class I woman, and 040, a class IIb man. The choice provides a contrast that, although not the most extreme that could have been chosen, allows a comparison of two quite different varieties of Glasgow speech. For example, speaker 045 has indices of 143, 135 and 107 for the variables (i), (u) and (au) respectively, and she used only 1 % glottal stops before a pause or a vowel. Speaker 040 has indices of 281,

275 and 345 for (i), (u) and (au), and he used 89% glottal stops before a pause or a vowel. The first ten minutes of the tapes were chosen to provide comparable samples. The frequency of tunes was calculated and the results are shown in table 19.[1]

Table 19. Frequency distribution of tunes
from two speech samples

Tune	Frequency 040	Frequency 045
(lower) mid to higher mid	46	6
low to (lower) mid	3	14
(higher) mid to high	1	1
low to high	1	3
(lower) mid to low	4	13
higher mid (or high) to mid	6	9
higher mid to low	1	15
high to low	1	3
mid to higher mid to mid	95	17
low to (lower) mid to low	4	2
mid to higher mid to low	3	10
(higher) mid to high to low	0	2
mid to low to lower mid	0	11
higher mid to (lower) mid to higher mid	1	4
higher mid to low to (lower) mid	0	12
mid to higher mid to low to lower mid	0	5
mid to higher mid to (lower) mid to higher mid	1	2
mid to high to low to (lower) mid	0	2
lower mid to low to lower mid	0	1
gradually down from (higher) mid: some, but not all, syllables of this tune may form a level succession	62	35
gradually down from lower mid	17	36
high or mid: if more than one in succession, each begins slightly lower than the preceding one	11	8
lower mid: if more than one in succession, each begins slightly higher than the preceding one	5	21
higher mid or high	1	2

It can be seen that 045's intonation is more varied; she uses a greater number of different tunes. 040's intonation has a tendency to prefer higher tunes and its regional character is typically shown by the extremely high frequency of high rise-falls. Although these

[1] See Macaulay and Trevelyan (1973, 234-40) for description of tunes and extracts of the analysis carried out by Dr W. Jassem.

do occur in Southern Standard English (differing probably sub-structurally, especially in the intervals used), they are here considerably more frequent. Even in 045's sample there are distinctly more such rise-falls than would be expected in Southern Standard English. Also, high falls are more frequent in 045's sample than they normally are in Southern Standard English. A striking difference between the two speakers is the extreme rarity of fall-rises in 040's speech. These tunes are employed by 045 in a manner similar to their use in Southern Standard English.

Although two speakers are too small a sample on which to base any far-reaching conclusions, the detailed analysis of intonation bears out superficial impressions. 045's speech is only slightly marked by local characteristics and it is possible that many observers would not immediately identify her as Glaswegian, although she would usually be recognised as a Scot. On the other hand, 040 is unmistakably Glaswegian, and one of the identifying features is probably the repeated use of rise-fall intonation. It is hoped at a later date to extend the investigation of intonation in the survey tapes and particularly to investigate age and sex differences in intonation. For the present, however, the analysis of the extracts from the two tapes shows that it is possible to make a meaningful comparison of at least one prosodic feature.

Comparison of Reading Aloud with Speaking

As part of the interview all the informants were asked to read some sentences aloud. The sentences contained a number of instances of the variables (i) and (gs), and it is thus possible to compare the average values for each of these variables in the sentences read aloud with the averages obtained from the rest of the interview.[1]

Table 20 shows that, with two exceptions, the general pattern of social stratification is the same in the sentences read aloud as that found in the rest of the interview. The exceptions are class I women and class I ten-year-old girls, both of whom show higher values in reading the sentences than would have been expected from the earlier figures, especially in comparison with class IIa women and class IIa ten-year-old girls. All groups, with the exception of class III men and class III fifteen-year-old boys, show lower values of (i) in reading aloud than in the rest of the interview. There are some interesting differences between the groups. Class I females show a very slight difference between speaking and reading aloud, whereas class I males all show lower values of (i) in reading, parti-

[1] Since one class III ten-year-old boy, 005, could not read, the average values for 034, one of the additional informants, are included in the totals instead. In addition, the results from one class III woman and one class III ten-year-old girl are missing because of faults on the tapes.

cularly the men and ten-year-old boys. In class III, on the other hand, men and fifteen-year-old boys actually have higher values for (i) in reading aloud than they do in the rest of the interview, although class III females all show lower values of (i) when reading aloud, particularly ten-year-old girls. However, perhaps the most significant finding is that all ten-year-olds, including class III boys, show much lower values of (i) in reading aloud than they do in speaking.

Table 20. Indices for the variable (i) from sentences read aloud, compared with the indices for the rest of the interview (in parentheses)

	I	IIa	IIb	III	All
All	161 (202)	175 (247)	220 (284)	263 (294)	205 (275)
Males	151 (224)	204 (279)	233 (287)	290 (300)	220 (273)
Females	171 (180)	146 (215)	207 (280)	236 (288)	190 (242)
Men	119 (189)	175 (269)	225 (305)	325 (301)	211 (266)
15-yr-old boys	203 (234)	244 (279)	275 (308)	307 (296)	257 (279)
10-yr-old boys	132 (250)	194 (290)	200 (248)	238 (302)	191 (273)
Women	144 (158)	132 (206)	244 (269)	238 (264)	189 (224)
15-yr-old girls	157 (163)	174 (219)	213 (279)	287 (319)	208 (245)
10-yr-old girls	213 (220)	132 (231)	163 (291)	182 (280)	173 (256)
All 10-yr-olds	173 (235)	163 (261)	182 (270)	210 (291)	182 (264)

The average values of (gs) in the sentences read aloud are given in table 21, with the averages for the rest of the interview in parentheses. Only in very few instances are glottal stops used before a vowel or a pause in reading the sentences aloud. Only class III men, class III fifteen-year-old boys, and class IIb fifteen-year-old boys use 50% or more glottal stops in reading aloud compared with the large number of glottal stops in speaking. As was the case with (i), the difference is particularly noticeable among the ten-year-olds, who used very few glottal stops in reading aloud.

As pointed out in chapter 3 the comparison of speaking styles with reading styles must be approached with caution, and since, in the present survey, the number of instances of the variables in the sentences read aloud is small, it would be unwise to place too great emphasis on the results. However, it is possible to draw some tentative conclusions. First of all, the importance of (i) as a social marker is confirmed by the reading results, although the pattern of stratification is clearer for males than for females. Secondly, almost all informants showed a shift towards the 'prestige' forms of (i) and (gs) in reading aloud. This is particularly marked in the case of (gs) and supports the earlier conclusion (and the popular view) that the use of glottal stops is a strongly stigmatised feature of Glasgow speech. Thirdly, the smallest differences between reading aloud and speaking occur among class I women and class I fifteen-year-old girls at one end of the spectrum of Glasgow speech, and among class III men and class III fifteen-year-old boys at the other end. These two groups represent the extremes of Glasgow speech sampled in the survey and the relative consistency in the use of the variables by these two groups is similar to Labov's findings

Table 21. Indices for (gs) before a pause and before a vowel from sentences read aloud, compared with the indices for the rest of the interview (in parentheses)

	I	IIa	IIb	III	All
All	5.0(30.9)	8.3(60.2)	16.7(79.7)	30.0(90.4)	15.0(65.3)
Males	3.3(30.9)	13.3(74.7)	26.7(80.0)	50.0(93.6)	23.3(69.8)
Females	6.7(30.9)	3.3(45.6)	6.7(79.4)	10.0(87.1)	6.7(60.8)
Men	0.0(11.3)	0.0(41.6)	10.0(89.1)	70.0(92.3)	20.0(58.6)
15-yr-old boys	10.0(25.0)	20.0(92.6)	50.0(81.7)	70.0(95.6)	37.5(73.7)
10-yr-old boys	0.0(56.2)	20.0(89.9)	20.0(69.4)	10.0(92.8)	12.5(77.1)
Women	10.0(9.3)	0.0(12.5)	20.0(66.4)	0.0(88.0)	7.5(44.1)
15-yr-old girls	0.0(24.8)	0.0(45.7)	0.0(77.8)	20.0(94.1)	5.0(60.6)
10-yr-old girls	10.0(58.7)	10.0(78.7)	0.0(94.1)	10.0(79.2)	7.5(77.7)

in New York, though it must be emphasised that the evidence from the Glasgow survey is fragmentary compared with Labov's.

Finally, the results for the ten-year-olds show a striking ability to approximate the 'prestige' forms of (i) and (gs) in reading aloud. If reading aloud were to be equated with a more formal speech style than that used in the rest of the interview, the results would suggest that the ten-year-olds are very sensitive to the social values that prevail in the adult world. However, there is an alternative explanation which may be more accurate. Judging from prosodic clues, reading aloud for most ten-year-olds is a very different kind of activity from speaking. In reading aloud the ten-year-old may be attempting to imitate his teacher in a classroom task, and satisfactory performance of this task may bear little relation to his ability to speak. The ability to read aloud 'correctly' may depend more upon a talent for mimicry than upon the internalisation of adult norms of speech. If this view is correct, and in the present state of ignorance about psycholinguistic processing it can be little more than speculation, then the results from ten-year-olds reading aloud serve more to cast doubt on the value of reading aloud as a 'speech style' than they do to support an optimistic view of the ten-year-olds' linguistic ability.

Other Linguistic Features of Glasgow Speech

The five variables that were analysed are not the only features of Glasgow speech that are socially stratified but, as pointed out above (p.28), they are the ones that lend themselves best to this kind of analysis, since they are relatively immune to conscious suppression. This does not mean that, for example, no instances of /e/ for /o/ were uttered during the course of the interviews. The following items were recorded (though only from class IIb and class III speakers): /ne/ 'no', /mer/ 'more', /mest/ 'most', /klez/ 'clothes', and /en/ 'own'. However, the number of such pronunciations was very small, much smaller than is regularly heard in everyday conversation with such speakers, thus confirming the suspicion that these speakers were inhibited to some extent by the interview situation. A few examples (also only from class IIb and class III speakers) of /a/ for /ɒ/ were recorded: /want/ 'want', /raŋ/ 'wrong', /əlaŋ/ 'along', /af/ 'off' and /waˀər/ 'water'. Several class IIb and class III speakers also used /o/ for /ɒ/ in certain words: /on/ 'on', /dʒob/ 'job', /boðər/ 'bother', /stopt/ 'stopped', /holɪdez/ 'holidays', /komɪks/ 'comics' and /pop/ 'pop'. Only four examples (all from two class III speakers) of the raising of /a/ to /ɛ/ or /e/ occurred: /dʒekɪt/ 'jacket', /feðər/ 'father', /ɛftər/ 'after' and /ebərdoniənz/ 'Aberdonians'. The following pronunciations were recorded only from class IIb and class III speakers: /wan/ 'one', /tʃʌɪndʒd/ 'changed', /masɛl/ 'myself', /pʌlt/ 'pulled', /pʌʃt/ 'pushed', /kɪlt/ 'killed', /stjupɪt/ 'stupid', /font/ 'phoned', /desənt/ 'decent', /dʒili/ 'jelly', /ɔ/ 'all', /sʌʊl/ 'soul', /aʊər/ 'over', /hɪŋk/ 'think', /polɪs/ 'police', /brɛks/ 'breaks', /kɒld/ 'cold', /dʌg/ 'dog' and /ʃudʒ/ 'huge'.

One pronunciation that is considered by many Glaswegians to be linked to religion did not show up with sufficient frequency to justify any conclusions. This is the use of /ɛr/ for /er/, which is said by some observers of Glasgow speech to be a distinguishing characteristic of Catholics. Only five examples were recorded from Catholics, four from one class III man and one from a class III boy: /ɛr/ 'air', /ðɛr/ 'there', /kɛrfɪl/ 'careful', /ɛriə/ 'area' and /ɛr/ 'Ayr'. However, one Protestant man used the form /pɛrɪnts/ 'parents'.

In addition to the pronunciations listed above the following items were recorded only from class IIb and class III speakers: /no/ 'not', /ˀe/ 'to', /fe/ 'from', /wʌr/ 'our', /wʌrsɛlvz/ 'ourselves', /hɪts/ 'its', /de/ 'do', /gi/ 'give', /giz/ 'gives', /firt/ 'feared' (=frightened), /wʌnst/ 'once' and /twʌɪst/ 'twice'.

At the other end of the scale, only three class I adults neutralised the vowels /ɪ/, /ɛ/ and /ʌ/ before /r/. All other informants kept the three vowels distinct before /r/ except when a low back variety of (i), which may be indistinguishable from /ʌ/, was used. Finally, none of the speakers distinguished *don* from *dawn* or *full* from *fool*, but they all kept *tide* /tʌɪd/ distinct from *tied* /taɪd/.

As for other aspects of language it was (with the exception of three examples from two class 11a speakers) only from class 11b and class 111 speakers that the following constructions were recorded: 'he has came', 'I seen the ship', 'I done it', 'I would've probably went for', 'they must've saw us', 'more than I used to could do', 'you done everything', 'I was going to lay up', 'I laid up', 'I'd've went down', 'it doesn't worry to me', 'my nose was broke', 'I used to didnae like them', 'my big brother got it to his birthday', 'I haven't went since', 'I should really have went', 'he was took to the police office', and 'my wife and I have fell out'.

Few informants used any local or Scots dialect words. The total list is as follows: *flit* 'move house', *chap the door* 'knock at the door', *ginger* 'soft drink', *check someone* 'scold', *birl* 'turn', *greet* 'weep', *wean* 'child', *a wee tait* 'a small amount', *jarries* /dʒɒrɪz/ 'marbles', *a whipping peerie* 'top', and *peevor* 'hopscotch'.

There was also the use of *dead* as an intensifier by both ten-year-olds and fifteen-year-olds: 'they're dead funny', 'she's a dead good teacher', 'it's dead slippy as well', and 'there used to be a dead big dog that lived up at our bit'.

The nature and scope of the interview did not permit an extensive investigation of vocabulary but all the adult and fifteen-year-old informants were asked if they knew ten 'old Scots words': *blether* 'a talkative person', *coup* 'to fall over' or 'a rubbish dump', *clype* 'to tell tales' or 'someone who tells tales', *scunner* 'disgust', *sneck* 'catch (on a door)', *fushionless* 'characterless', *oxter* 'armpit', *thole* 'endure', *blate* 'shy', and *tim* 'empty'. The informants were asked if they knew the word and what it meant. Only those informants who could give some idea of the meaning were counted as knowing the word.[1]

All the adults were familiar with *blether*, *coup*, *clype*, and *scunner*; only one class 1 man did not know *sneck*, and only one class 11b man did not know *thole* (though his wife knew it). Only one class 1 woman and one class 111 woman did not know *oxter*. Six informants (five of them women) did not know *tim*. Only three informants (all class 1) knew *fushionless*, and only two informants (one class 1 women and one class 11a man) knew *blate*.

The responses from the fifteen-year-olds were very different. The only word that they all knew was *blether*, though all but three knew *clype*. None of them knew *fushionless*, *blate*, or *tim*. Only one class 1 girl knew *thole*; the other class 1 girl knew *sneck*, as did one class 111

---

[1] It is possible that some informants did not recognise a particular word because of the interviewer's way of pronouncing it.

boy, but none of the others had heard it. The numbers who were familiar with the other words are as follows: *coup* 5, *scunner* 10, and *oxter* 6.

The average number of words known by the adults was 7.8, and by the fifteen-year-olds, 3.3. This suggests that some of the words, e.g. *thole*, *tim* and *sneck*, are being lost and this view was confirmed by the adult informants who often remarked that such words are rarely heard nowadays. It is also perhaps significant in this connection that the glossary of Glasgow gang slang in Patrick (1975) contains very few traditional Scots words.

Conclusion

The conclusion from the evidence presented in this chapter is that the linguistic variation displayed in the Glasgow survey (mainly in the five phonological variables) is systematically related to social class and sex, and that the pattern is less clear at the age of ten though it is fairly well established by the age of fifteen. No clear indications of systematic variation according to differences of religion were found. The nature of the social class differences will be further examined in the next chapter.

5. Social Class

We never went without, but we didn't have three-course
meals and things.

023, class 11b woman

SINCE WIDESPREAD disagreement exists among socio-
logists with regard to the nature of social class, it is hardly surprising that sociolinguistic surveys have used different methods for
determining social class (see Macaulay 1976 for an account of the
differences). In the Glasgow study, occupation was chosen as the
criterion for social class membership for a number of reasons. In
the first place, information about occupation is relatively easy to
obtain, and it is not as potentially embarrassing a topic for
informants as questions about family income. Secondly, since the
schools usually have a record of the father's occupation, it was
possible to select informants through the school records; this
allowed the selection of a balanced sample to proceed much more
quickly than would otherwise have been the case. Thirdly, there
was no recent demographic survey of Glasgow that would have
provided the necessary basis for weighting other factors contribut-
ing to social class distinctions. Fourthly, occupation is generally
regarded as the best *single* indicator of social class (Barber 1957,
Glass 1954, Parkin 1971).

The four-way classification of occupations used to select the
sample was arrived at by taking the three-way distinction used by
Kellas (1968) in his study of Scotland, and dividing his second
group into non-manual and manual classes. This latter division
was made because the non-manual/manual distinction is generally
considered one of the most important social class differentiators in
a modern industrial society (Goldthorpe, Lockwood, Bechhofer
and Platt 1969; Parkin 1971).

In chapter 4 it was shown that, in the case of five phonological
variables, the considerable variation that occurs in Glasgow speech
is systematically related to the social class groups selected on the
basis of occupation. It is also apparent from the analysis that there
are sex differences, in that for each social class the women generally
show lower indices than the men. Whether this is because women
are generally 'better spoken' in terms of the prestige forms than
men, or because husband's occupation is a less accurate indicator
of social class for women, is hard to determine.

Given the small size of the sample the regularity of the results is quite remarkable and underlines the systematic nature of linguistic variation. However, because of the small numbers of speakers involved, and because similar patterns were found for all

Table 22. Rank order of all the speakers, based on the sum of the indices for the four vowel variables

No.	Class	Employment	Sum
a) Men			
050	I	Director of family business	670
015	I	Depute head teacher	678
010	IIa	Tax officer, higher grade	969
028	IIa	Policeman	1012
040	IIb	Radial-arm driller	1169
032	IIb	Electrician	1238
027	III	Cleansing department worker, recently promoted to supervisor	1238
048	III	Lorry driver	1248
b) Women			
045	I	Civil engineer's wife	505
030	I	Physician's wife	553
019	IIa	Commercial artist	710
036	IIa	Salesman's wife	884
023	IIb	Blacksmith's wife	1110
047	IIb	Electrician's wife	1139
054	III	Factory worker	1200
044	III	Fruit market porter's wife	1205
c) 15-yr-old boys			
004	I	Consultant dental surgeon	870
049	I	Director of family business	931
011	IIa	Tax officer, higher grade	974
029	IIa	Policeman	1115
026	IIb	Machine shop engineer	1127
001	III	Labourer	1139
041	III	Fruit market porter	1267
024	IIb	Blacksmith	1281
d) 15-yr-old girls			
031	I	Doctor	676
037	I	Depute head teacher	706
020	IIa	Commercial artist	722
051	IIa	Sub-editor	1060
052	IIb	Joiner	1105
025	IIb	Radial-arm driller	1176
002	III	Boilerman in public baths	1215
042	III	Lorry driver	1278

four vowel variables, it is possible to look beyond the group means to the rank ordering of individuals on the basis of their use of these four variables. Since similarly constructed indices were calculated for each variable, it is possible to sum these indices to produce a composite score for the use of the four vowel variables. For example, speaker 050 has an index of 185 for (i), 163 for (u), 143 for (a) and 179 for (au), which gives him a composite score of 670 for the four variables. By the use of this rather crude measure, it is possible to rank order the speakers.

Table 22 shows that among the adults there is not a single individual out of place according to the order predicted on the basis of occupation. The only possible anomaly is the equal ranking of 032 (class IIb) with 027 (class III). The results for the fifteen-year-olds show one boy (024) out of place, but the results for the girls are as predicted. Only among the ten-year-old girls, where there are three anomalies (022, 016 and 053), does the prediction break down slightly. With these four exceptions (and the deviations are all by a single rank), the composite scores on the four vowel variables correspond exactly with the ranking on the occupational scale for all informants.

Even though the sample is small the consistency of the results is impressive in two respects. In the first place, it shows how the evidence from a small number of phonological variables can 'place' a speaker on a scale relative to other speakers from differ-

Table 22—*continued*

e) 10-yr-old boys

009	I	Lecturer in further education	843
021	I	Chief draughtsman	873
013	IIa	Draughtsman	975
014	IIa	Engineering inspector	989
035	IIb	Security guard	1058
018	IIa	Electrical engineer	1121
007	III	Lorry driver	1193
004	III	Unemployed labourer	1211

f) 10-yr-old girls

046	I	Civil engineer	761
012	IIa	Collection salesman	896
022	I	Managing director, whisky bond	937
008	IIa	Salesman	962
033	III	Labourer	1129
016	IIb	Electrician	1151
006	III	Slater, roadmender	1151
053	IIb	Machine shop engineer	1185

ent social levels. Secondly, it offers support for the view that occupation would prove a useful indicator of social stratification. However, what the linguistic evidence does not fully support is the view that the informants would fall into the four classes according to which the sample was chosen. The indices for all five variables show the smallest differences occurring between class IIb and III, suggesting that it may have been wrong to treat them as distinct classes. If the results for these two classes are combined, as shown in table 23, the differences between the groups become much more clearly marked.

The only place where the results from the different groups are at all close is in the figures for glottal stops. However, the use of glottal stops is the most highly stigmatised feature of Glasgow speech and a common subject for overt comment and jokes. Informant 019, a class IIa woman, is the only person in the sample who uses no glottal stops and thus seems to exhibit a clear example of what Labov (1966b) has called hypercorrection. With this exception, the three social class groups are seen to be clearly distinguished by their use of five phonological variables.

Of course, these are not the only features that distinguish the speech of the informants. As was shown in the previous chapter, class IIb and class III speakers are more likely to use dialect forms and constructions than class I and class IIa informants, though it would be hard to distinguish further between the classes. On the whole, since dialect words and constructions were fairly rare in the context of the formal interview, the phonological variables are probably a more reliable measure of linguistic variation for this particular sample of Glasgow speech. On the other hand, the fact that the dialect features occur only in the two lower social class groups may be taken as support for considering them as a single class, and the fact that dialect features do not occur in the interviews with the other two social class groups suggests that the boundary between the two lower social class groups (IIb and III) and the other two social class groups is not simply an artifact of the phonological analysis.

Since the grouping of classes IIb and III together runs counter to the original expectation that the two groups would be distinct from each other it would be helpful to find supporting evidence. In order to explore this further it is necessary to look at how the informants perceived the situation. Four questions were put to the adult informants in connection with social class divisions:

People often talk about there being different (social) classes—do you think this is true in Glasgow?

How many classes would you say there were in Glasgow?

Where would you put yourself in a class system?

60

Table 23. Average indices for all five variables by class, with classes IIb and III combined. (gs) percentages rounded to the nearest whole number

	(i)			(u)			(a)			(au)			(gs)		
	I	IIa	IIb, III	I	IIa	IIb, III	I	IIa	IIb, III	I	IIa	IIb, III	I	IIa	IIb, III
All adults	174	238	285	145	212	303	133	201	260	152	247	348	10	27	84
Men	189	269	303	157	224	311	143	228	264	186	271	348	11	42	91
Women	158	206	267	132	199	294	123	174	257	117	222	348	9	13	77
All 15-yr-olds	199	249	301	192	237	306	165	200	249	242	286	345	25	70	88
15-yr-old boys	234	279	302	223	256	304	182	223	249	263	287	349	25	93	89
15-yr-old girls	163	219	299	160	217	308	148	176	248	221	285	340	25	46	86
All 10-yr-olds	235	261	280	200	255	305	176	169	234	244	272	332	58	85	84
10-yr-old boys	250	290	275	199	242	304	171	173	233	239	278	334	56	90	81
10-yr-old girls	220	231	285	201	268	305	180	164	235	249	266	329	59	79	86

What is it that determines which class you belong to—family, education, money, or job?

The responses to these questions provide a commentary to accompany the indices listed above. Any comments or questions from the interviewer are printed in italic.

The lorry driver (048), who comes at the bottom of table 22a, described himself as 'just your ordinary working chap, struggling for a living', while the electrician (032), who comes slightly lower than predicted in table 22a, described himself as 'just working class – I certainly don't fancy myself as a snob, I'd hate to think it.' On the other hand the cleansing department worker (027), who had recently been promoted, was very conscious of his position:

Oh, well – oh, I'm just a – well, I think I'm – I'm as good as anybody else, but – eh – I mean I don't behave like – well, I behave the way I feel – eh, you know, I don't try to put anything on of a – because I've got a good – better job now. I think we're doing OK. I'm still the same the same fellow I was before, you know. I still go with the same pals and things like that, go to the football, stand on the terrace, and – that, you know. I mean I wouldn't think of going to the stand because I've got a better pay now, you know. *If somebody called you middle-class, would you be surprised?* Eh, aye, I suppose I would be. I don't really believe in that middle, class, you know, myself, to be honest.

The remaining informant in the bottom half of table 22a (040) was outspoken about where he put himself: 'Right at the bottom of the heap.' Yet when pushed he admitted:

We're doing not too bad, you know, because the fact that – eh – we're cautious. Both my wife and myself, we tend to realise that – eh – the old standards as far as – they're still maintaining in quite a lot of communities and quite a lot of – eh – our class. Whereas – eh – the drink, bingo, smoking, and these sort of things, these play a big part. These are to them in the working class are the opium that they manage to get through this harsh life with, but not with us. We realise that we concede these things for the – the bits of leisure and pleasure that we've got here at the moment.

Similar responses were obtained from the women informants. One of the class III women (044) identified herself as working class while the other (054) responded: 'I don't consider myself in a class; I just live up to what I was brought up to.' Both the class IIb women (023 and 047) identified themselves as working class, but the latter observed:

... the likes of Cranhill, Ruchazie, Barlanark all these places, they're mostly all working-class people, that have, like myself,

got on a wee bit, you know, that I'm a – as I say, an awful lot
better off than I was, when I lived in Parkhead, because my
family were all young, and – eh – as I say, my husband's an
awful hard worker. If he didn't work as hard as – eh – as he
does – well, I wouldn't have the wee bit comfort that I have
got for myself and my children.

023 also was aware that she was better off than some: '. . . as you go
further up the scheme you see right poor people.'

The picture that emerges from the comments of the class III and
class IIb informants is that although there are distinctions at this
level, basically there is only one class. These are the responses from
the lower half of tables 22a and b. Moving up table 22a produces a
much less clear picture. 028 remarked:

I don't know where I'd place myself really, I'm just a worker
really. *If someone called you middle class would that be all
right?* That might. Aye, it could do, I suppose.

010 classed himself as working class, but in context it is obvious
that he is using the label in a rather special sense. In answer to the
question about the number of classes in Glasgow he replied:

Well, there's the very poor who are knocking their head
against the ceiling all the time, and there's the other ones who
are just managing to get along. There's the real labouring
classes who are making big money and then there are the other
ones who are in jobs and are making that more money, and
they come into places where they can buy houses and into
areas where they're accepted money-wise but I wouldn't say
socially. And you've got the cream, as you call them, more or
less the professional class and I think even there I use the term
working class. I would class myself as working class but we're
– how would you put it? – the real – eh – not the professional
class.

It is difficult to know exactly how to interpret this statement, but
it is reasonably clear that he placed himself between 'the real
labouring classes' and 'the professional class'. Similar kinds of
responses were obtained from the two class IIa women. 036 said
that she would place herself 'not very high up – I'd say sort of
middle class', and 019 was even more explicit:

Well I wouldn't call myself middle class but on the other hand
I would call myself middling. In other words, I'm not up there
and I'm not down there. I just reckon I'm pretty average.

Thus all four IIa informants seemed reluctant to label themselves
middle class, though they gave indications that they occupied an
intermediate position between the high and the low.

The class I informants similarly rejected any suggestion of being
upper class, though their responses revealed that they did not see

themselves as occupying an intermediate position in the way that the class 11a informants did. 015 refused to put himself in a class:

> I'm quite indifferent what class I'm in. *But if someone said you are upper class, would you agree with that?* No, I would just say I was a professional man, that's all. I work with my brain, and I'm prepared to work with my hands also ... I don't know how I'd place myself.

050 also rejected the label upper class and claimed to be middle class:

> *Well, if you're middle class, where's the upper class?* In Glasgow? Oh, if we're talking about Glasgow, I honestly don't know because again we've been relatively fortunate. We can move within any society in Glasgow at all. We've no problem on this level. *So you really are upper class, though you wouldn't ... ?* No, I wouldn't like to be described as that at all. *But, in fact, there isn't a higher level that you're conscious of?* Oh, there probably is, in fact. There's probably a level which is higher . . . generations of families who have lived within the counties and so on but ... they're a small number. They don't concern us from the point of view that we can still and do meet them and we can meet them on precisely the same terms that we would meet people from a lower or what one might describe as a lower class of society.

045 took an even more exalted view of the class above her:

> *Where would you put yourself?* Well, I suppose middle class – if people talk about the middle class. *Well, if you're middle class, is there an upper class?* Well, the upper class I always feel is the royalty or sort of aristocracy. I always think of them as the upper class, which is, I suppose, the old opinion, you know, of it, but I do feel that they still rank as the upper class. *Would you say there were many upper class people in Glasgow?* I would say mostly middle and working class, then, from that point of view.

030 also claimed to be middle class:

> *Not upper class?* No, because my husband once laughed at me for calling myself upper middle class. (Laughs) That's the only reason. *Where's the upper class in Glasgow, if it's not you?* No, I don't think there's a class in Glasgow which is noticeably higher than the kind of – em – area that we have here.

Note that even when making this last admission 030 could not bring herself to state it in terms of people but transformed it euphemistically into neighbourhood.

Several conclusions can be drawn from this set of comments by the informants. In the first place, they tend to support the claim that occupation is a valuable indicator of social class. Secondly, the comments indicate that the informants were aware of their own social position, although they did not always find it easy to put it into words. Thirdly, the informants' responses suggest a tripartite division of the population into an upper, a middle, and a lower class, whatever labels are attached to them. This probably does not include the whole range of social differences in Glasgow. At one extreme, there is a level higher than the 'upper class' but their numbers are relatively small. At the other extreme, there are the 'very poor' that are also not represented in the sample, and whose numbers are presumably larger than those of the 'upper-upper class'. Nevertheless, the informants' comments suggest thst the tripartite division into social classes revealed by the linguistic variables is consistent with the perception of the informants themselves. In other words, the results suggest not only that the speech of Glaswegians varies along a continuum closely correlated with social differences but also that Glaswegians indicate their membership in one of three social classes by the way that they speak. This class identification through speech lends support to the view that social class membership is a psychological as well as an economic phenomenon (Centers 1949).

The use of occupation as the sole indicator of social class appears to be justified by the results, but there are certain caveats that must be noted. In the first place, the average age of the adult informants was 48 (range 32 to 72), so it is reasonable to suppose that they had all reached a stage where their occupational status was unlikely to change radically. The inclusion of a group of adults in the twenty to thirty age range might have complicated the use of occupation as the sole criterion for social class membership. Secondly, Glasgow's economy has been stagnant or declining since the end of World War I (see chapter 2), and this may have contributed to reduced social mobility. Thirdly, the sample was extremely small. In a larger sample, the use of additional information on income, education, type of residence, etc., might have proved useful in helping to determine social class membership. However, the use of multi-dimensional scales is not without its problems (see Macaulay 1976).

Finally, although the sample is too small to draw general conclusions from the responses to most of the questions, the answers to one of them show an interesting range, which is worth illustrating because of the implications for the educational system. The question was: What do you think it takes to get ahead in life?

The class III and class IIb informants again form a group. They tended to emphasise luck or natural ability:

> Ambition and a lot of luck. If you get the break and you're there at the right time, this is what counts. (032)

You've got to have a – more so at this level, you know, you've got to have a flair for something, you've got to be a – either have this artistic thing that – eh – makes you good with a ball or – you can somehow manage to fit in with a pop group, start singing or that. These sort of things are instantaneous success. If you have this natural flair, then you'll – you have the passport, as it were, to this level where we all strive to get to, or most of us anyway – or – you take the hard slog through the educational system, which as I said to it already we didn't realise it was necessary. *Looking back on it what do you think of the kind of schooling you got?* Well, I daresay that – that – that the schooling at that time was – was adequate but – eh – my own approach towards it because of the environment that I came from was one of sheer apathy and indifference. I thought that schooling and all education was just a shackle imposed upon you something that you had to do because you had no option. It was forced upon you and – eh – as I say, consequently, I couldn't get out of it quick enough, but I know now that – eh – that was a sad loss at that time. *Did any of your friends think differently?* No, I think they all shared the same opinion that – eh – school was just something imposed upon you. (040)

The class IIa informants were slightly cynical:

Eh – I would say a brass neck. Definitely confidence in – eh – a confidence in yourself and also – um – I would say – something I don't like and something I can't be and that's just – um – a disregard for others. (010)

Cheating. And – and brass neck, really. But there are others who get ahead by good hard work and being honest and reliable and – and those ab- – who are above them see this and the opportunity then is opened out to them. (019)

The class I informants stressed character and education:

Well, they – of course, there is fundamental education and there is – eh – character and balance – eh – a person must subdue his emotions, no matter how trying things may be he's – he's got to keep them down, he's got to be efficient to do a job well and stick at it. He must stick at the thing and – I would generally say – make – make oneself indispensable. (015)

Now, do you mean if they go in from university, from that angle, or . . . ? *Or in general to be successful, what kind of qualities are needed?* Well, I think nowadays it is essential to have – em – a good secondary education and the exams are – you've got to sit them, you've got to pass them, you've got to have degrees, to get on in a lot of things now. You can't get in to them unless you have 'Highers' and a university degree. But

I think that's necessary, but even apart from that I think you have to have the initiative yourself, to decide the type of thing you want to get to do and then go for that sphere. (045)

This range of responses shows that those who had been relatively successful in their lives tended to emphasise the control that an individual may exert over his own destiny, whereas the others looked for explanations external to the individual. However, it was one of the class IIb informants who eloquently expressed what he saw to be the basic class difference:

When I was younger, I didn't know – I didn't realise the power – eh – of teaching your kids, I thought that parents were just here to bring kids into the world and to – to give them sufficient benefits to get by but it's been brought home to me now that you've got to be feeding a kid more than one way. When they're young you – you just sort of – at our level, we feel that if you just give them three squa – square meals a day, then you're feeding them. That's OK. But I – I realise that that's not true now. I realise now that – eh – parents who have a great insight into the educational system know that you don't talk down to a child. You speak to it as an adult. You try to nurture and bring it along and – eh – this makes a great platform for a child. When it goes to school and – eh – when it starts to circulate in other social groups, then it's got this start, that – eh – the working class child hasn't got because he's been shoved aside all the time. He's had to make his own experiments and draw his own conclusions. They haven't been passed on from parents. (040)

The same point was made more succinctly, but almost as effectively by the informant who comes lowest in table 22a:

What do you think it takes to get ahead in life? An awful lot of good luck. *Yes. Anything else?* Well, I think you've really got to be pushed by your parents. Unfortunately, we don't all allow our parents to push us and we sort of rebel again, and that's you out. (048)

6. 'Standard English'

See, I'm not really broad Glasgow but when I go to England, you know, it sticks out much more than it does in
Glasgow.

046, class I ten-year-old girl

IN ACCOUNTS OF sociolinguistic situations in Britain and in
the United States, there is probably no term that is more frequently
used and less clearly defined than the expression 'Standard English'
(see the discussion in Macaulay 1973). It is often suggested that
there are great disadvantages in not being able to speak Standard
English: '. . . being relatively happy and successful in the middle
and upper reaches of the English-speaking world requires the
ability to use Standard English' (Brooks 1964, 26). '. . . it is necessary to teach standard English to non-standard speakers (because)
it is necessary to know *the language of the country* if they are to
become part of the mainstream of that society' (Barataz 1970, 26,
emphasis added). If a knowledge of Standard English is as important as these quotations suggest then it is essential to make quite
clear what is meant by the term. One example (Wolfram 1969, 17)
will illustrate the kind of definition usually given or implied:

> Standard English is defined in this study as a socially accepted
> variety of English established by a codified norm of 'correct-
> ness'. Non-standard English is defined as any variety of
> English which differs from this established norm.

There are several problems with this kind of definition. Wolfram
speaks of *a* socially accepted variety of English rather than *the*
socially accepted variety, suggesting that there may be more than
one. However, he does not tell us by whom the variety is accepted
or where to find the codified norm of correctness. Without this
information the 'definition' is totally vacuous since it is self-
evident that every variety of English is socially acceptable at some
level. If it were not, it would not be a variety of English but simply
the idiosyncratic speech of a single individual. However, it may be
unfair to Wolfram to take his words literally. Probably most
readers would assume that he meant the implicit norm in the
speech of the educated minority, which is partially codified in
grammar books, dictionaries, and phonetics textbooks. Although
it may seem a definition of the *lucus a non lucendo* type to define a
standard on the behaviour of a minority, the practice is too widespread to cause surprise.

However, it is the second part of Wolfram's statement that is more significant. He says that nonstandard English is defined as any variety of English that differs from the established norm. It is not simply a quibble to ask: How great must the differences be for the variety to be considered nonstandard, and are all kinds of differences equally important? In particular, it is essential to determine to what extent lexical, grammatical, and phonological differences are involved. Much of the work on black English in the United States (e.g., Labov *et al.* 1968, Wolfram 1969, Fasold 1972) has, in fact, devoted considerable attention to phonological processes and the classification of speakers as standard or nonstandard has been largely on differences in pronunciation. This is in contrast to Abercrombie (1965) who suggested that Standard English should not be defined with reference to any one form of pronunciation, no matter how prestigious. However, it would be wrong to imply that phonological differences are totally irrelevant to a definition of Standard English, if for no other reason than that many people believe that they are important. The problem is that there is no single standard which applies to pronunciation. The difficulties involved can be seen in the following quotation (Crystal 1971a, 34):

> The mark of an educated person, it has been said—and this is true to a very considerable extent still—is that by listening to him you cannot tell which part of the country he comes from. And it would clearly be ludicrous to expect someone with a very broad regional accent to make a success of a job as a High Court judge.

The first part of this statement is manifestly untrue, in spite of the parenthetical disclaimer. While it is true that some educated people in England have nonlocalised accents it is not true that all or even most educated English people show no regional characteristics in their speech. And if the scope of the question is widened to include Ireland, Scotland and Wales, not to mention the United States, Canada, or Australia, the idea of a single standard of pronunciation becomes absurd. In fact, all 'standards' of pronunciation are, to some extent, parochial and the problem that must be faced is how to determine the standard for a particular region. The question raised by the second part of Crystal's statement is: What is meant by 'a very broad regional accent'? The intensifiers are, in themselves, a contradiction of Crystal's first assertion, since he is clearly not confident that a *regional* accent or even a *broad regional* accent would prevent someone, presumably 'an educated person', from becoming a High Court judge; only a *very broad regional* accent would do that. But who is to decide on the breadth of a regional accent? Is it the outsider or the members of the regional speech community? The answer to this question is not so obvious as it might appear, because it is sometimes suggested that one of the criteria of a very broad accent is that it is unintelligible to outsiders. However, there are obvious dangers in allowing outsiders to determine what is 'acceptable' with a speech community. A cautionary example can be given from a recent book on teaching spoken English (Harvey 1968, 12):

> Speech that is characterised by such qualities as flatness of tone, paucity of speech tunes, little muscular effort in the use of lungs, lips, jaw or soft palate, may reasonably be considered inferior to speech that makes full and flexible use of the speech organs . . . The local speech of all the great conurbations is often characterised by the misuse, or underemployment of the speech organs in the ways given above. It is on this account that there are few to sing the praises of the accent of, for instance, Birmingham or Glasgow. There is a case for regarding such urban accents as debased.

The author even has an explanation for the existence of such debased accents (p.6): 'For it can be readily observed that city dwellers often make only partial use of their speech organs, their breathing being shallow and their muscular agility weak.'

The harshness of this judgement may be so distasteful to many people that it can best be countered by another quotation in a totally different tone (Mackay 1882, 2–5):

> The English bristles with consonants. The Scotch is as spangled with vowels as a meadow with daisies in the month of May. English, though perhaps the most muscular and copious language in the world, is harsh and sibilant; while the Scotch, with its beautiful terminational diminutives is almost as soft as the Italian. . . . the Scoto-Teutonic has an advantage over the old Anglo-Teutonic and the modern English, in having reserved to itself the power, while retaining all the old words of the language, to eliminate from every word all harsh or unnecessary consonants. Thus it has *loe* for love; *fa'* for fall; *wa'* for wall; *awfu'* for awful; *sma'* for small; and many hundreds of similar abbreviations which detract nothing from the force of the idea, or the clearness of the meaning, while they soften the roughness of the expression.

The contrast between these two quotations illustrates, as is obvious to most people, that value judgements about language are subjective. This does not mean that such judgements should be ignored. On the contrary, they form the basis of the social reality in which members of a commodity live and must be understood if we are to attempt an explanation of any aspect of that community (Schutz 1967). However, it is the values that prevail inside

70

the community that are important, not the ill-informed prejudices of outsiders. Absurd physiological explanations of the kind put forward by Harvey reveal a complete ignorance of the complex psychological and sociological factors involved in linguistic choice. Although the study of language acquisition is still in its infancy there is already convincing evidence that all normal children are incredibly proficient in acquiring linguistic skills (Lenneberg 1967). There is no reason to believe that the range of linguistic variation in a large conurbation is the result of differences in linguistic ability at an early age, and the number of individuals that change their speech in late adolescence or early adulthood suggests that many more people would be capable of changing their speech if they wished to do so.

In attempting to characterise 'Standard English' in Glasgow, there are four questions that must be considered:

1. Are there widespread differences in language in Glasgow?

2. If there are such differences, do the differences correspond to divisions or groupings within the community?

3. Are there any grounds for labelling the language of any group or groups 'standard' and that of any other group or groups 'non-standard'?

4. If so, what does it mean to attach such labels to the language of a group?

The material presented in chapters 4 and 5 provides considerable evidence for affirmative answers to questions 1 and 2. Even within the restricted scope and formal style of the interview, there are wide differences among the speakers and certain of these differences correlate closely with social class, age and sex. Most of the differences are phonological although there are also some differences in the use of dialect forms and constructions. The evidence of social class differences is clear enough, but it is far from obvious how to relate this evidence to the standard/nonstandard distinction.

If we look at the group results for the phonological variables alone the informants fall into three classes, not two (see chapter 5), and there are no obvious *linguistic* grounds for drawing the line between standard and nonstandard speakers. If on the other hand, we look at the individual indices for the phonological variables (pp.58–9 above), the informants can be rank ordered on the social class dimension but again there is no obvious linguistic point at which the standard/nonstandard line can be drawn. In neither case do the phonological variables provide an easy way to dichotomise the sample of Glasgow speakers into standard and nonstandard.

However, it may be a mistake even to attempt to do this. Trudgill (1974), for example, is quite emphatic that phonological differences should not form part of the definition of the standard language. If

71

we agree with this view, then we are left with only a small number of dialect words and constructions by which to divide up the sample of Glasgow speakers into standard and nonstandard. Since it is only the class IIb and class III informants that use such forms this would be easy to do, but it is much harder to decide what significance such a division would have. In the first place, the number of dialect forms is very small in any single interview and thus it may be largely accidental whether a particular sample of speech contains any examples or not. Consequently, even if this view of the standard/nonstandard dichotomy is adopted, it seems wrong to label the total output of these informants as nonstandard English. For the most part, by this definition, they are speaking standard English, except for the intrusion of a few nonstandard forms. Secondly, it is clear that within the city itself, few of these 'nonstandard' forms would cause any difficulty of understanding to the informants, whose speech would be considered standard by this criterion. In fact, it is interesting that it was the class I and class IIa informants that were most familiar with the traditional Scots vocabulary (see p.55). Thus while it may make sense to label certain linguistic forms 'nonstandard' because they are not normally *used* by educated speakers or news broadcasters (Trudgill 1974, 17), this should not imply that such forms are not widely understood throughout the community. If this is all that a distinction between standard and nonstandard English in Glasgow amounts to, then it is hard to see why it should be granted much importance. Such differences are no more (and no less) important than differences in pronunciation, as far as communication is concerned.

It is time to consider the fourth question raised above: What is the significance of labelling the speech of one group 'standard' and that of another group 'nonstandard'? The answer begins to seem obvious: it is an easy way of concealing prejudice about socially stigmatised forms of speech under the guise of academic respectability. If standard English is 'the variety which is normally spoken by educated people' (Trudgill 1974, 17), the use of nonstandard English may be interpreted as revealing a *lack* of education. If education is viewed as 'formal initiation into the linguistic prejudices of the middle class' (Sledd 1969, 1307), then this interpretation may not be completely wide of the mark. But if education is seen as a process of intellectual development and the acquisition of knowledge, then the *use* of nonstandard (or socially stigmatised) forms of speech is irrelevant. It is not the past tense forms of irregular verbs that are important for intellectual development but the *meanings* of the words that are in the vocabulary of any educated person. It is when a ten-year-old remarks that he does not know what 'nationality' means that he reveals that he is not yet a

72

speaker of standard English, not when he says 'I done it' or 'I seen it'. Carol Chomsky (1969) and Piaget (1959) have shown how easy it is for adults to overestimate the child's understanding of adult language, and Barnes (1971) illustrates the problems many children will face in school because of their teachers' failure to realise this. Any characterisation of nonstandard English on the basis of the use of a few dialect forms (or on the basis of pronunciation) can only distract attention from the real problem in the schools, which is to increase the pupils' knowledge and understanding of the language that they all speak, namely English without any qualifying epithet.

Since the term 'standard' by use and through its other connotations has become synonymous with 'correct' (i.e. socially approved by the higher class), it may be necessary to adopt an alternative label for the form of English that is used and understood by all educated people. The obvious candidate is Common English, deviations from which would be examples of Uncommon English, which they often are in the case of dialect expressions, though none the worse for that. Such a re-labelling might help to put the controversy over correctness in language into perspective.

Finally, it is essential not to forget that the primary purpose of language is the communication of meaning. This can be illustrated with a rather homely metaphor. Drinking vessels come in many shapes and sizes and are made of diverse materials, from crystal goblets and silver quaichs to tin cups and plastic containers, and, other things being equal, we often prefer one to the other. But, in the final assessment, the drinking vessel is unimportant compared with the quality of the liquid it contains, for it is not the cup itself that quenches our thirst but what the cup holds. The grammatical structure of language can be seen as parallel to the shape of the drinking vessel and pronunciation as parallel to the material of which it is composed, and both of these can be judged aesthetically, independently of each other. What the cup can contain is meaning. If we are thirsty we are likely to be more interested in the quality of the drink than in the shape and composition of the cup. Similarly, with language the criterion of value rests in the effective communication of meaning rather than in choice of grammatical form or pronunciation. There are two further parallels. First, there is the appropriateness for a particular situation or function, and it is important to remember that this is largely a matter of convention. You may be very proud of your Wedgwood fine bone-china teacups, but your friends would be surprised if you served champagne or brandy in them. Secondly, what is appropriate in one situation may not be so in another. Going mountaineering, a tin cup may be more serviceable than a china teacup. Similarly, with language there is no reason to expect one variety to be the most appropriate for all situations or for all functions, which is why we all change our style of speech frequently. Everyone knows this, and yet it is surprising how often it seems to be forgotten.

7. Responses to Glasgow Speech

> There was nothing wrong with people who spoke school
> English all the time, but they were a little cut off from real
> life, or suffering from pretentiousness, or maybe just
> foreigners who didn't know.
>
> Cliff Hanley (1958, 19)

ALL THE fifteen-year-olds and adults were asked to respond to
short taped examples of Glasgow speech, which were collected
during the exploratory interviews conducted in 1970 and 1971.
The technique used was based on that used by Labov in New York
(Labov 1966, chapter XI).[1] Twelve short samples of speech were
played and the informant was asked to evaluate the speaker in
terms of background and occupation. Originally it was intended
to record the responses of the informants on tape to allow as free
as possible a response, but technical problems with the second
tape-recorder prevented this from being carried out with all but a
few informants. Instead, the informant's responses were written
down by the interviewer. This had two limiting effects on the
elicitation of information. First, the informant's responses were
restricted to what could be taken down in longhand by the interviewer with the risk of some editing in the process. Secondly, and
probably more important, the interviewer's attention was dis-
tracted from prompting the informant to provide more detailed
information. Despite these limitations, the consistency of the

[1] It would perhaps be less misleading to say that the idea for this part
of the interview came from Labov than to claim that it is based upon his
approach in the New York survey. Labov used passages from a standard
reading in which sentences read by five speakers were presented to the
informants in mixed order. It was not possible to do this in the Glasgow
survey because no materials of this kind were available. Instead, extracts
from the exploratory interviews were used. The disadvantage of using
examples of actual speech is that it is impossible to be certain what it is
that the informants are responding to in making their judgements, since
content may be as important as speech quality. On the other hand, the
use of oral readings instead of speech introduces a risk of distortion
since reading aloud is a quite different activity from normal speech. The
use of oral readings by Labov (1966), Giles (1970, 1971), and Frender
and Lambert (1973) allows a much more rigorous interpretation of the
results than is possible in the Glasgow survey, but it is only by inference
that their results can be extrapolated to actual speech and it is possible
that this inference is unjustified. The choice between the use of oral readings and using examples of actual speech presents a real dilemma for the
investigator of judgements about language.

responses provides clear evidence of the ability of the informants to categorise their fellow citizens by their speech. Moreover, the recording of the informants' responses in their own words provides more information than the rating on a one-dimensional scale that Labov used, though this information has to be interpreted for tabulation, with the risk of distortion by the interpreter.

The twelve passages were taken from the tapes recorded by eleven people, as follows:

1. Working-class male, aged 40
2. Working-class female, aged 35
3. Working-class male, aged 60
4. Working-class female, aged 19
5. Middle-class female, aged 35
6. Working-class male, aged 18
7. Middle-class female, aged 65
8. Middle-class male, aged 50
9. Same as 3
10. Middle-class female, aged 70
11. Middle-class female, aged 19
12. Middle-class male, aged 19

The same speaker occurs as 3 and 9, but in two very different samples from the same interview. It had originally been intended to use this technique in more examples of the present investigation but it proved too difficult to get satisfactory contrasting extracts which were of a high enough acoustic quality to be used, with the result that only one example remains. However, the different responses to examples 3 and 9, as will appear, show that it is possible for the same speaker to be rated differently according to the style of speech he is using.

The responses to each sample will be presented in the next section and in the section after that the general pattern of responses will be examined. The responses were interpreted in terms of the occupational scale used in selecting the sample of informants, i.e., classes I–III. However, it should be stressed that the informants were not asked to use a four-point scale and in some cases their responses were difficult to assess.

1. Working-class male, aged 40, employed by the Glasgow Corporation as a garage inspector. Grew up in the Gorbals, left school at 15.

> They wear long hair. I mean the Corporation says you're not supposed to have long hair. *Yes.* They tell you not to have long hair. *Yes.* They tell you not to have long hair but (gs–1) I mean, nowadays (au–4) it's (i–3) a waste of time – I mean, I admit (i–4) myself nowadays (au–3) it's (i–3) a general trend. I mean everybody wears – you either wear it (i–4) long or you

don't but, ehm, these are one of these things (i–3). But I wouldn't like my own son to have long hair.

Speaker 1 shows high values for (i) and (au), and his intonation is characterised by marked rise-falls.

Most of the informants unambiguously categorised speaker 1 as class III, e.g. manual worker, labourer, shipyard worker, factory worker, navvy, bus conductor, bus driver. Only three informants suggested that he might be at the level of a skilled worker. One IIa father said that he could be 'a man in my own position', while one class III boy thought that he could be a teacher.

2. Working-class female, aged 32, born in Govan, left school at 15, married to a merchant seaman.

Ach well, I don't think they really talk any different (1–3) from us only got that wee bit (i–5) (gs–1) of twang, (a–2) the same thing as my mother-in-law and them from Kilbirnie – when they come up – they've always got that wee bit (i–4) (gs–1) of different (i–3) twang (a–2) you know, 'ye ken' and 'ye know', and that (gs–1) you know. But (gs–1) up here if you say 'ye ken' they would think (i–3) you're off your head [af yər hid] or something (i–4).

Speaker 2 shows very high values for (i) and consistently uses glottal stops.

Almost without exception the informants categorised speaker 2 as class III. One IIa boy said she was a cleaner 'because most of them speak like that'. The only exceptions were a class III boy and girl, who thought that she might be a skilled worker's wife.

3. Working-class male, aged 60, grew up in the Calton, served in Merchant Navy during the war, works 'in the rag trade'.

I liked America. It was a novelty, (gs–0), America, you know, but New Zealand was a fine country. *So I believe*. Oh, a beautiful (gs–0) country. The only thing (i–3) I didn't like about (au–4) New Zealand, uh, in the towns (au–3) after six (i–2) o'clock at night – it's bad (a–2) enough here after six (i–2) o'clock at night but there in Auckland and Wellington – I travelled right round (au–3) about (gs–0) (au–3) it, (gs–1) you know and Dunedin – after six (i–2) o'clock you couldn't (u–2) buy a packet (a–2) of cigarettes, (i–2) everything closed up.

Speaker 3 shows quite low values for (i), (u), (a) and (gs) but fairly high values for (au).

The responses to this speaker were very varied, and importantly so because he occurs in a quite different style as speaker 9. Only three informants classified him as class III. The majority perceived him as IIb but almost as many considered that he could be middle class. Three informants suggested that he might be a teacher, two

77

others a ship's officer, and a 11a boy thought he could even be a doctor. These perceptions, as will be seen, differed greatly from those of the same man in his other guise as speaker 9. However, almost as interesting as a contrast with 9 is the range of responses to this sample. It was clear that speaker 3 was much harder to 'place' than 9. Some of the higher responses to speaker 3 may have been influenced by the subject matter, believing that only someone reasonably well-off would be able to travel. However, of those who realised that he might have been a sailor only one suggested that he was an ordinary seaman.

4. Working-class female, aged 19.

> When I was at school, (u–3) when I done anything (i–1) I used to get hammered for it, you know. If I'd to come home [hem] and telt all these stories I'd get hammered for it but the rest of them – a lot (gs–1) of them just got (gs–1) away with it (gs–1) but (gs–1) I never got away with nothing I used to get hammered good (u–3) for it (gs–1).

Speaker 4 shows high values for (u) and consistently uses glottal stops. She also speaks very quickly in a staccato style.

Almost all the informants categorised speaker 4 as belonging to class 111. There were only three exceptions: a 11a boy suggested that she might be married to a clerk, a 11b boy considered that she could be an office girl and a 11b mother said that she might be 'a housewife, something like myself'.

5. Middle-class female, aged 35, grew up in Townhead, of working-class parents, left school at 14, wife of a technical manager in an engineering firm.

> They're just not (gs–1) interested (i–1) I mean, I don't work and if I don't go out (au–2) (gs–1) and clean up and wash down (au–1) the stairs and all these sort (gs–1) of things (i–1) they wouldn't (u–2) be done. You know, I mean, the people were cleaner, I think, where you were.

Speaker 5 shows low values for (i) and (au) but twice uses glottal stops before a following vowel. She also uses a noticeably fronted dipthong [æ^ɪ].

Speaker 5 produced a wide range of reactions. Only one informant categorised her as class 111 and that was a class 111 girl whose judgements were often out of line with those of her peers. None of the class 1 informants considered that she belonged to the middle class, they all categorised her as 11b. However, the working-class informants rated her much higher, including being a doctor's or a manager's wife. Three informants described her as 'Kelvinside', 'Kelvindale', and 'Kelvingrove', terms which can be considered as equivalent although it is 'Kelvinside' that is the usual label for a stereotyped affected accent. Other informants suggested that 'she things she's something, thinks she's higher than she really is', 'trying to put on airs or graces'.

6. Working-class male, aged 18, grew up in Barlanark, left school at 15, unemployed, unskilled worker.

> No, no really, but, (gs–1) then again, you go across the road into Easterhouse (au–4) and that (gs–1) and fight with the boys over [auər] there. No, but, now (au–4) – now (au–4) it's getting (gs–1) too bad (a–3) and that (a–3) (gs–1) you know, they're all pulling [pʌlɪn] blades or something like that (a–3) (gs–1).

Speaker 6 shows high values for (a) and (au) and consistently uses glottal stops. He speaks very quickly in a staccato style.

This speaker was generally consigned to a low status: manual worker, labourer, unemployed, bus conductor, street sweeper, 'works on a building site'. Some were even more condemnatory: 'layabout', 'bottom of the heap', 'wee ned from Easterhouse', but a few considered that he might be a young apprentice. Only one 11a boy thought that he was middle class: 'good education, good job, perhaps a schoolteacher'.

7. Middle-class female, aged 65, grew up in Kelvinside.

> Yes, I think (i–1) so, because we had to have friends to enjoy our company and we used to go in parties, (gs–0) to dances and parties (gs–0) to various houses, (au–2). It was in one house (au–3) one month and someone else's house (au–2) the next month.

Speaker 7 shows intermediate values for (au) and uses no glottal stops. She speaks slowly with rather breathy voice quality.

Speaker 7 was generally recognised as middle class and typical comments were 'slightly higher class than clerk', 'not got all that much money but not working class', 'respectable older woman', 'Oxfam worker', and 'nice speaker from good class district in Glasgow'.

8. Middle-class male, aged 50, civil servant.

> I was just reading the Herald this morning and even Sir Alec (a–2) Douglas-Home had some plan (a–3) for Scotland that never has come to anything (i–1), yet you feel that (gs–1) – delegation to Scotland for Scottish (gs–0) affairs, it might help things. It's a big (i–1) question of course.

Speaker 8 shows very low values for (i) and intermediate values for (a). He speaks slowly in a very low-pitched voice.

Speaker 8 was the highest ranked by all social class groups except the class 1 group, who rated him considerably lower than speaker 10. A number of informants, perhaps influenced by the topic of the extract, suggested that he was a politician or a councillor. This view was put most clearly by a class 1 girl: 'stays in

Bearsden, just moved there from Glasgow, bowler-hatted, umbrella type, perhaps to do with the Council or in Civil Service'. Only two informants, both middle class, suggested that he might be working class.

9. Working-class male, aged 60, same as speaker 3.

There was an old women (u–3) in with an umbrella [ʌmbərɛlʌ] like, you know, she'd be over sixty (i–2). So she started shouting (au–4) (gs–1) at him: 'Don't you use that language (a–2) here. You's are not (gs–1) in Glasgow. You's are not (gs–1) in the Gorbals', and that (a–3) (gs–1) you know. 'Ach', he says, 'you shut up, you old hag, (a–3).' So she hit (i–5) (gs–1) him over the head with the umbrella.

Speaker 9 shows high values for all the variables.

In contrast to the estimates of the same man as speaker 3, almost all informants classified speaker 9 as class III: manual worker, labourer, navvy, nightwatchman, brickie, road sweeper. Only a few considered that he might belong to class IIb. However, all informants rated speaker 9 considerably lower than speaker 3.

10. Middle-class female, aged 70, daughter of a stockbroker, educated at private schools and Glasgow University, a retired doctor.

On the other hand, I can remember my great friend and I used to come home and say to Isa, 'You know, I don't know, I don't know what Jess is supposed to do (u–2). Because sometimes when she says a thing (i–2) somebody'll say to her "Why didn't you think" (i–2) and then she'll say something (i–1) else and somebody says to her "Who told you to think" (i–2).' I said, 'What (gs–0) are you supposed to do (u–2)?'

Speaker 10 shows fairly low values for (i) and (u). She also uses a fronted diphthong [æɪ] and speaks rather slowly and deliberately.

Speaker 10 was rated differently by the various social class group. The class I informants rated her highest of all the speakers. The class IIb informants also considered her to be class I, but lower than speaker 8. The other two groups generally judged her to be class IIa though there were exceptions. One class III informant considered her to be class I and another rated her as class III. None of the IIb informants judged her to belong to class I, and one IIb informants rated her as IIb. Two IIb and two class III informants said that she was not a Glaswegian.

11. Middle-class female, aged 19, grew up in Coatbridge, daughter of a civil servant, first-year medical student at Glasgow University.

Thumbs up, that (a–3) was it (gs–1). I'd forgotten (gs–1) you went like that (gs–1) (a–3) and said, 'Thumbs up, a minute' (i–2) that's right (gs–1) uhuh. Do you know I was just listening

80

(i–1) to a – looking at a programme (a–1) on television the other day and there was a lot (gs–1) of little (i–2) girls and one would say, 'OK' and they all, they all shouted, (gs–0) 'No het, (gs–1) no het', (gs–1) and I just suddenly remembered that – we used to do (u–2) that too, when we were small.

Speaker 11 shows fairly low values for (i) but consistently uses glottal stops.

Speaker 11 was generally considered to be middle class, though a sizeable minority of informants judged her to be IIb. Only one informant suggested that she might be at university, though two others said she might have attended a training college.

12. Middle-class male, aged 19, grew up in Govanhill, a first-year student at Stirling University.

As I grew older sort of – all these sort of gangs (a–3) sprouted up again, you know, because, for a long time the gangs (a–2) were non-existent. *Yes.* They they sprouted up again, so it directed it formally, you know, things like Catholic and Protestant, they just got a gang (a–2) versus gang (a–2). Now, it's actually – a lot (gs–1) of the gangs (a–2) have – although – it's not less violent – a lot of the gangs (a–3) have disappeared (i–3). It's sort (gs–1) of – it's no longer sort (gs–1) of organised violence as it was for – you know when I was, say, fifteen (i–2) sixteen (i–2) – it was a very big (i–1) thing (i–2) gangs (a–2) then. In the last two years the differences (i–2) is tremendous, a lot quieter (gs–0). So the violence is now individual (i–2) you know.

Speaker 12 shows fairly high values for (a) and (gs) but lower values for (i). He speaks rather softly with creaky voice quality.

Speaker 12 was generally considered to belong to IIb, an apprentice learning a skilled trade. However, five informants did suggest that he could be a university student.

For the purposes of tabulation a four-point occupational scale, similar to that used in the selection of informants, was used. Occupations in class I were rated 1, those in class IIa were rated 2, those in class IIb were rated 3, and those in class III were rated 4. The responses to each sample speaker from each social class group were summed and averaged (see Macaulay and Trevelyan 1973, 93–110, for details). All four social classes showed similar patterns of response. The fifteen-year-olds, in particular the boys, rated speakers 3 and 8 higher than the adults. The boys also showed the greatest contrast in their judgements of the speaker who appears as 3 and 9: all four classes rated 9 much lower than 3, but the boys ranked speaker 3 at 2 on the occupational scale, compared with a rank of 2.8 from all other informants. One possible explanation for the difference between the boys and the other informants is that at that age the boys are less aware of the values of adult society than are the girls.

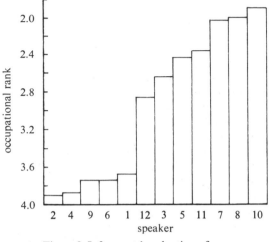

Figure 8. Informants' evaluation of average
occupational rank for each speaker

However, the differences in the responses of the informants are less important than the overall similarities. In spite of the difficulty of isolating what it is that the informants are responding to in the samples of speech,[1] it is clear that the informants share a set of values by which they can evaluate their fellow citizens on the basis of very short stretches of speech. The average ratings for each speaker on the tape are shown in figure 8. It can be seen that there is a clear division into at least two groups, with speakers 2, 4, 9, 6 and 1 forming a single group distinct from the others. Also, although the distinction is not so great, there is a difference between the group composed of speakers 12, 3, 5 and 11 and that made up by speakers 7, 8 and 10. This is consistent with the tripartite social class division described in chapter 5, and, with the exception of speaker 3, corresponds to the ranking of the speakers on an occupational basis. Speaker 3/9 shows how the judgement of an individual can vary according to the form of speech he is using. In view of some of the comments by teachers and employers

[1] Although the nature of the tape does not justify drawing conclusions about what informants are responding to, it is significant that speaker 11 is rated fourth highest in spite of the fact that she consistently uses glottal stops before a pause or a vowel. If any of the five phonological variables is responsible for the difference in judgements, the nature of the responses suggests that it may be (i), though this needs to be tested under more rigorous conditions.

in chapter 8 it is perhaps significant that speaker 3/9 had spent some time away from Glasgow.

8. Attitudes towards Glasgow Speech

If you live in Glasgow you must talk like a Glaswegian.
011, class IIa fifteen-year-old boy

IN THIS CHAPTER the attitudes towards Glasgow speech of informants from all three sets of interviews will be presented. Because this is an area in which the possibility of misrepresentation and misinterpretation is very great, the views of the informants will be presented mainly through their own words and with a minimum of interpretative comment. The implications of the attitudes shown in this chapter will be discussed in chapter 9.

1. The Community Sample

Only the adults and the fifteen-year-olds were asked about language in the interviews, and the majority thought it was a good thing that people in different parts of the country speak differently. Among the reasons given by the fifteen-year-olds were the following:
a) it makes speech more interesting:
> It would be boring if you couldn't tell the difference between people. (004, class I)

b) it is nice to hear different kinds of speech:
> It's nice to hear people speaking differently. (029, class IIa)
> Yes, because it gives a change of voice. (051, class IIa)

c) it gives individuality to speaker or culture:
> It identifies people. (031, class I)
> Oh yes, it gives them individuality. There'd be absolutely no character if everybody was alike. It's just the same as different nations, only on a smaller scale, the same with even their currency, you know the different currency. It all adds to, you know, each unique culture, I would say. (037, class I)
> Yes, if you all spoke the same way, you couldn't call anyone Scottish, Irish or Welsh. It would all be English. (011, class IIa)

Those fifteen-year-olds who thought it wasn't a good thing that people from different parts of the country spoke differently, gave as reasons:
a) it impedes understanding:
> I don't think so really, because if you go down to, say, Lancashire and you come from up north, you won't have a clue what some of the people were saying. (020, class IIa)
> No, not really, because if you go to a different part of the

country, say in the north country of England, you couldn't understand a word they were saying. (026, class IIb)

b) it would be better if we all spoke 'proper' English:

It would be a good thing if we all spoke the same. *In what way?* You need to speak proper English, proper English that gets spoken at school. (041, class III)

Seven of the nine fifteen-year-olds that approved of regional accents belonged to classes I and IIa; four out of the five that considered regional accents a disadvantage were from classes IIb and III.

The adults advanced the same sort of arguments for and against dialects:

a) that they make speech colourful or varied:

Yes, it's much more colourful from the language point of view to have different dialects. I enjoy very much listening to the different parts – I can't identify them all by any means – but I like hearing the differences. (030, class I)

Yes, it's quite nice, you get the variation just as the flowers are different colours, quite nice. *Do you think it would be a bad thing if we all spoke the same?* I wouldn't say it would be a bad thing, no, but it's nice to hear the different dialects. (019, class IIa)

b) that they give individuality to people:

Well you need variety. You need to have people talking their own way, English or Scottish. It gives them . . . it gives them individuality. (010, class IIa)

In disagreement, that regional accents made it difficult for people to understand one another:

It makes it harder an awful lot of times for folk to understand, I just cannae understand a Geordie, I don't suppose a Geordie can understand me, mind you. I find most Englishmen that come up with the servicemen, I've got to ask them to repeat what they're saying, I just cannae pick up their twang. (032, class IIb)

But generally the adults were less categorical in their opinions than the fifteen-year-olds. They saw that dialect was not subject to control:

It's just dialects, that's what it is. (028, class IIa)

There's not much you can do about it. (032, class IIb)

Individual answers raised more than one point:

Well I'm all for letting them have their local dialects, yes I'm quite interested in the dialects and so on, although I would like to see a standard, a more standard form of English. It's very difficult, for example, to understand people in remote parts of Aberdeenshire and so on, they speak quickly. And I remember being down in Cork several years ago taking a walk in the country and I went into a pub with my wife, into a country pub, and people were talking there, several men, and I said to the landlord later when they went out. 'Is that Irish they're speaking?' and he said, 'Oh no, that's the Cork dialect'. Well it was completely incomprehensible to me, but . . . oh no, I think I would let the dialects be preserved. (015, class I)

To tell you the truth I've never really given it a thought. I find some of the English people I can't make them out and that, of course a lot of the English can't make the Scots out so it's all one, you know, but I really haven't given that much thought at all. Sometimes it can even be fun trying to like . . . trying to find out where a person comes from through listening to their voice. (047, class IIb)

Five out of the eight adults that approved of regional accents were from classes I and IIa, whereas the two that disapproved were from classes IIb and III.

Most of the informants agreed that one could always recognise a Glaswegian by the way he speaks, though this claim was sometimes qualified in one of three ways:

a) it is difficult to distinguish the Glaswegian speech from the regional west coast of Scotland speech:

Do you think you can tell someone from Glasgow by the way he speaks? Yes, I think so. I don't notice it in conversation with people live but if somebody's broadcasting on television or something you at once register the Scottish, Glasgow intonation. I don't know that I could pick out Glasgow as distinct from anywhere else in the south-west of Scotland. (030, class I)

Well not so much Glasgow, I think the West of Scotland you can, you know, there's a lilt to them and you can tell the Highland lilt and the Irish. (028, class IIa)

b) that it depends on what part of the city the person comes from:

Yes, I think so, well it depends what part of Glasgow they come from. (049, class I)

It all depends on what part of Glasgow he comes from. Again, I mean, you know, like me you could tell right away that I come from Glasgow, I've got I suppose a Glasgow twang – I don't think I've got a Glasgow twang, but. . . . (032, class IIb)

c) only if it is a really broad Glasgow accent:

I suppose so. Well, I suppose if you've got a really broad Glasgow accent you can, but then again, I think you could recognise somebody from Edinburgh if they had a broad Edinburgh accent. (037, class I)

Although both the adults and the fifteen-year-olds could and did

86

distinguish between different varieties of speech in Glasgow, only four of them believed that it could be said with some certainty which particular part of the city a speaker came from.

> *Do you think you can recognise someone from Glasgow by the way he speaks?* Yes, probably. *What about the part of Glasgow he comes from?* Well I don't know if I would recognise it, I think it probably could be recognised by someone from the same district, not so much as recognising that you come from Glasgow. (036, class 11a)

> *Can you tell what part of Glasgow someone comes from?* Oh no, no' really. There's maybe an odd part, you get some people from Gavingad, well it's Royston now well certainly hearing some of them talk you can tell, you know, but apart from that. . . . (027, class 111)

> Well I could probably tell whether they came from Glasgow or this area [Whitecraigs] assuming that they didn't go around wearing the same dress as the boys in Glasgow do and talk the same way. (049, class 1)

> Some places you can tell where the people come from, but not all the time. *What kind of places?* Castlemilk, you can tell someone that comes from Castlemilk. *How would you know?* He'd sort of speak all slang. *Any other places?* No, I'd say that's about all. (051, class 11a)

The others who did contrast speech areas of the city talked on terms of extremes, contrasting Kelvinside with Gorbals or Govan.

> *Could you distinguish between different parts of Glasgow?* Oh yes, yes I think there's still a bit of a Kelvinside accent and a bit of the . . . perhaps the west end and the south side are more similar than they used to be, and certainly the folks in the Gorbals are very different again, I can certainly distinguish a broad Glasgow accent with no difficulty. (040, class 11b)

These represent socio-economic extremes as much as different parts of the city, and some of the adults specifically mentioned class differences:

> *Can you distinguish between parts of the city?* No, no, you wouldn't – well you could only again if you're talking in terms of class but not in terms of similar people moving to different parts of the city, there's no difference in accent from one part of the city to another generally. (050, class 1)

> *What about different parts of Glasgow?* Well you've got the toffs and as you say, the middle class, the working class, but you still know they're from Glasgow, you know what I mean. (044, class 111)

Since the majority of fifteen-year-olds and adults thought: a) that regional accents were a good thing; and b) that a Glaswegian could be recognised by his accent (although the part of Glasgow he came from could not be specifically predicted), and that Glaswegian was a distinct regional accent and one that gave them identity, one would expect it to follow that they approved of Glasgow speech and were self-confident in their use of it. However, in rating their own accent the fifteen-year-olds and some of the adults showed a lack of confidence in the Glasgow speech.

When asked if they thought that the way one spoke affected one's chance of getting a job, eleven of the fifteen-year-olds agreed with this statement, four thought it mattered for some jobs and only one thought it did not matter. Those who thought it did matter mentioned certain varieties of accent or speaking 'well':

> *Do you think it matters how you speak for getting a job?* Yes, I would say so. *For all jobs?* I think your whole appearance must be . . . I think you would have to look efficient, you'd have to be competent, you'd have to sound competent. Do you mean accent? *Yes.* Your accent – well, I suppose again it's just bias, but they tend to look for somebody who's got a Kelvinside accent, or something, rather than somebody who's got a much broader accent. (037, class i)

> Well I think if you talk in a broad Glasgow accent you're less likely to get a job than somebody from a slightly higher class area. (049, class i)

> Oh yes, the language you use as well, that really counts. *In what way?* Well, if you go in swearing nobody would want to have you. *But other than swearing?* Well you're maybe wanted for a job that requires you to speak and so your speaking would really count. (020, class iia)

> If you speak well and you're well-dressed, they're more likely to give you the job. *Do you think that's true of all jobs?* Most jobs. (051, class iib)

> *In what way does it matter how you speak?* Well, in the way you speak, the way you dress, the way you act. *Do you think that's true for all jobs?* Mostly all jobs, I suppose. (052, class iib)

Those who thought it mattered for some jobs, mentioned different kinds of jobs:

> *Do you think it matters how you speak for getting a job?* In some cases, yes, I suppose it does. *What cases?* If you were . . . something like banking or something. They'd probably prefer you to have a purer kind of speech. (031, class i)

> *For all jobs?* Not for all of them, just for some. If you were going into an office to be a typist or something, well you've got to be social and that, you've got to be able to speak nice. (002, class iii)

> *For all jobs?* Especially shops and that, not work in a factory

or anything like that. In shops. (042, class III)

The one fifteen-year-old who said that it did not matter how one spoke for getting a job was a class III boy.

Having said that the way you speak is important for getting a job, a majority of the fifteen-year-olds said they would change the way they speak in order to get a better job; in classes I, IIa and IIb three out of the four fifteen-year-olds said they would change the way they spoke, but in class III only one fifteen-year-old said she would. However, those who said they would be willing to change the way they spoke did qualify their statements in certain ways:

a) if it was not going to affect them socially:

> *If you could get a better job by changing the way you spoke, would you do so?* If I felt that it wouldn't make any differences to my life or anything like that. Well, if I felt that it wasn't going to harm me in any way, you know, I would try to. *What kind of harm would it do?* Well, like lose friends, maybe some of your friends wouldn't like you because of the way you talk, that's probably unusual but . . . apart from that then I would, yes. (049, class I)

b) depending on the job:

> I don't know, it would have to depend on the circumstances, what the job was and if I liked it or not. (029, class IIa)

c) if it were possible:

> Well, I'd try, try my hardest. My parents are all for me changing the way I speak, they're not very happy about it, because there are certain words I can't pronounce properly, or won't. (025, class IIb)

The dilemma was brought out most clearly by a class IIa fifteen-year-old boy who, when asked if it mattered how you spoke for getting a job, said:

> I think it does. If you were an employer and somebody came in to see you in a broad Glasgow accent and then another boy, man, came in with an English accent, you'd be more inclined to give the English man the job because he had a nicer way of speaking.

But when he was asked if he would change the way he spoke by sounding like an Englishman in order to get a better job, said:

> I don't know that I would. I wouldn't like to have an English accent. I think it's a very daft one. They pronounce words correctly but they don't sound very nice. In your own environment you'd feel out of place. If you live in Glasgow you must talk like a Glaswegian, but not to the extent of broad Glasgow. (011, class IIa)

The adults were not asked directly or indirectly to evaluate their own speech (although one class IIa adult did do so of his own

89

accord), but were asked if there was anything they didn't like about the way people round about them spoke. Of the five class I and class IIa adults asked this question, all expressed a negative attitude towards Glaswegian speech, or forms of it:

Oh, it's the slovenly speech in the industrial areas I don't care for. No, it's like the Belfast accent, you probably heard that on the television – I detest that accent, and these industrial cities, I don't like the accents they have. (015, class I)

Yes, again are we talking about Glasgow or are we talking generally? Well, Glasgow. I'm not terribly fond of the Glasgow accent because I think it's a . . . it's lazy, just as I think I'm not fond of Scouse – it's lazy. These are basically two accents I'm really not terribly fond of. (050, class I).

Is there anything you don't like about the way the Glasgow people speak? Yes, the very broad accent. I'm not talking now about – it's when it's 'you's' and the usual ones they have. I think they could be a bit more, sound more, they could be educated and yet speak, keep their accent. (010, class IIa)

It's a bit long drawn out, isn't it? We have certain words we drag out like that. Yes, I don't say it's very nice really, it isn't nice. And when I hear it on television I say, 'Oh-h-h'. *Do you like the way the Edinburgh people speak?* No, no. There's no doubt either the Inverness or the Highland people or the English really have us beaten here. Their speech is much preferable to ours. (019, class IIa)

Well, I say I don't like it. I say I don't like the very broad way they speak, some people speak, but I suppose, that's a slightly snobbish attitude. (036, class IIa)

The one person who did comment on his own speech rated himself on a class-pronunciation scale and expressed a negative response to his own way of speaking:

Do you think it makes a difference how you speak for getting a job? I think it does, yes. I mean I'm not a speaker as you can see. I don't . . . I'm just a common sort of, you know I'm not . . . I've often wished I'd gone to some sort of elocution lessons because I meet so many people in my job and I feel as if I'm lower when it comes to speaking, you know. (028, class IIa)

Three class IIb and class III adults who were asked the question showed that they were aware of the same critical attitude towards Glaswegian speech as the class I and class IIa adults, but implied or affirmed different standards for their own speech.

Do you think it makes a difference how you speak for getting a job? Oh yes, definitely. Another thing I've also found out . . . I'll admit I'm not polite but see if I'm saying anything to Tricia I'll speak to her polite. But I find when they go to the big schools, the senior secondary, it's as though it's cissy to speak polite, that's what I find. Because in fact the oldest boy, the one you saw that day, he can be a nice speaker, but you wouldn't get Gerard to speak polite because I think the way Gerard looks at it, that, 'Oh, he'd be a right Jessie if . . .', you know. That's the honest . . . and I don't think you hear so many nice speakers. My two oldest girls were lovely speakers when they were young but I find that when they got to the senior secondary that they seem to change and in fact their words are slang, they definitely are slang. (047, class 11b)

Probably for some jobs but I don't really see that it should. If you know what you're talking about you should be able to talk the way you like, I don't mean talk ignorantly, but as long as you know what you're talking about. I mean, you see some of these fellows on the television and they've got good jobs some of them just talk away quite natural, you know, they don't try to put anything on, but I suppose it does help you right enough in some jobs. (027, class 111)

Well a lot of people don't like the Glasgow dialect, the way I'm speaking just now, you see they don't like that at all, that's not proper English. This is the way we've always spoken. (039, class 111)

2. The Teachers Sample

The interviews on which the following section is based might better be termed 'conversations', in that the points discussed depended more on the interests and experience of the informant than on the pre-selected questions, and, in addition, the interviewer did not refrain from expressing his own views. Moreover, as the series of interviews proceeded certain points which had not been raised in earlier interviews began to assume greater importance. In spite of these variations in conducting the interviews, much of the same ground was covered and the central issues were always the importance of language for the pupil's future success and the extent to which the school was meeting the pupil's needs.

One question that was raised with all the informants concerned the importance of pronunciation or 'accent'. Almost all of the teachers were aware of a range of accents in Glasgow, but they differed considerably in the way they responded to the issue. The extent to which they thought that accent was important was generally shown by the extent to which they thought that the school should attempt to influence the way the children spoke.

Exactly half the teachers in all three categories, and half the teachers in each of the separate categories, thought that the school should not attempt to change the pupils' accents. From primary school teacher to university lecturer almost identical sentiments emerged:

> The emphasis should be on getting children to use language meaningfully. The pronunciation thing is not of first importance. (T30, primary school teacher)

> As long as people are articulate, as long as they know what they're trying to say, it doesn't matter what sort of accent they use. (T08, secondary school teacher)

> The question of accent is secondary, if what is said is well considered, if it makes use of the full resources of the language. (T01, university lecturer)

Almost a third of the informants thought that the school should attempt to influence the way the children spoke, and the extent of concern (in terms of numbers) correlated with the level at which the teachers taught and the consequent involvement with the speech of their pupils. Those least concerned about accent were the university lecturers. The teachers who thought that the school should do something described what they did themselves:

> Yes, my own method is to correct the child when it makes a speech fault. I do try to get a good standard of English. In fact I would exaggerate ... speak more slowly, articulate more clearly. I try to get the children to raise their standard. (T19, primary school teacher)

> *Do you feel the need to point out faults of pronunciation?* Yes. *Why?* It does sound better. You can understand what they are saying much better. (T21, primary school teacher)

> You should set an example, but not an unattainable one. But you would need to show that their language isn't acceptable at all times. (T10, secondary school teacher)

> *What kind of things would you criticise in their speech?* All the basic Glasgow defects which we all have in our speech. The glottal stop, the tendency to run words together, the narrow range of vowel sounds. (T23, secondary school teacher)

> At the time I was using a tape recorder quite a lot. It's something I don't like to do to children, say to them: 'Don't speak like that you've got to speak properly', this kind of thing, because it's always said of Scottish children that they are reticent, they don't have that much to say. If you're going to deal with them that way, you're going to make them more introverted. ... I was interested in tape recording and we did a news programme. I would go round different children and then I would play it back and I always made sure that within the little group of about five or six I had somebody I considered spoke well comparative to the rest of the group. ...
> You would point out when someone said something well. You

92

found others saying, 'Can I do my bit again', because you found them wanting to do as well as the other child. (T40, college lecturer)

There was also a small group of informants concerned about the social importance of accent, the fact that certain accents are more socially prestigious than others. They thought that the school should not correct accents, in the way the other teachers had suggested, but that the issue of accent should be discussed in school and that the part the school should play would be to offer different models so that the children could modify their accents if they so wished.

Do you think that accent is trivial or important? I think it is important that people understand that the question of accent is an unscientific one. It's a question of aesthetic preference and social snobbery. It's got nothing to do with the quality of language whatever. It's very important that we teach this as an overt concept to children. It really is most tragic that some children think they speak bad English merely because of the type of accent they use. . . . People talk about ugly accents and things like that. It really is astonishing. Very difficult to handle that one. But I think it is important and I go out of my way to say that accent is by far the least important facet of your linguistic characteristics. It's one that doesn't affect your performance for any reason except people's assumptions. I also try to get across the idea that modifying your accent as linguistic tact is not hypocrisy. It's common among the tough section to retain their accent unmodified. The attitude is a pity and in fact the people who do say this do modify their accents without knowing it. (T38, secondary school teacher)

As to the first question [changing the way children speak], that is an emotive one in many quarters. I would return to my safe position and say that everyone has two registers. The gradual adoption of the more carefully enunciated register ought to be encouraged. . . . But the teachers must tread warily so as not to give offence. Point out that there are advantages in developing the second register from a purely mercenary point of view. (T41, college lecturer)

These informants showed the same inconsistency in attitude with regard to regional accents in general and Glaswegian as an example of a regional accent as some of the adults in the community sample did. Although most of them said that they liked regional accents and that they would not like to see them disappear, slightly more than half of them said that they did not like the Glasgow accent or some forms of the Glasgow accent, and negative statements about it were frequent:

The accent of the lowest state of Glaswegians is the ugliest accent one can encounter, but that is partly because it is associated with the unwashed and the violent. (T01, university lecturer)

I think some people tend to be snobbish about speech and I think people look down on Glasgow speech, as heard on TV, and our accent is broad compared to some parts of the country, but I think it's just people's attitude towards it. (T22, primary school teacher)

I dislike some of the Glasgow speech but then I think it is a speech problem rather than anything else. There is a kind of speech – a great resonance, but it sounds awful. There is also a nasal accent – but these are personal feelings. (T39, university lecturer)

My parents, for example, were critical of slovenly Glasgow speech. Neither of them belonged to Glasgow. They tended to think that Glasgow speech was something to be avoided at all costs. (T34, training college lecturer)

There were also some favourable comments about the vigour and homeliness of Glasgow speech, but they were much less common than the adverse remarks. (A summary of the informants' comments is given at the end of the chapter.) Although they do not say so explicitly it is probably a fair interpretation to suggest that when the informants affirm the value of local accents they are thinking in terms of regional identification and when they deplore 'careless' or 'slovenly' speech they are concerned about social distinctions in language. There were also numerous comments on the difference between the language used in the classroom and that used outside:

They ought to learn different forms of speech in different situations. It's something we all do unconsciously and I feel that the way they speak is fine for the schoolyard situation and another way of speaking for the classroom situation. (T24, secondary school teacher)

This situation is often referred to in terms of two languages or bilingualism:

I think they've got two languages. In school they're not as bad as they are outside. It's up to the teachers to encourage them even in their outside speech, but then the parents sometimes speak even worse than they do, so there's not much you can do about it. (T21, primary school teacher)

They do speak two languages, we found that. When they go out in the street they speak a different language. (T13, primary school teacher)

This school presents most problems in terms of speech. This

is environmental because the children speak two languages, Glaswegian amongst themselves – and even in the classroom it's difficult to get them to talk English. (T28, primary school teacher)

Most children have their outside language and their school language. Here they are reluctant to speak English. They will speak in Glasgow dialect. They are unused to speaking English and they become embarrassed. *Does that limit their ability to communicate in the classroom?* Very much so, especially if you come here expecting them to speak English and insist on it. (T10, secondary school teacher)

Small children haven't learned to differentiate the social relationships, but as they get older they do speak with a different mode to the adults. This makes them bilingual. I think this is the difficulty that the kind of children we have, have a difficulty of translation, that they've really got to relearn a language. It's not a case of language development but to relearn a language. (T30, primary school teacher)

The informants were all aware of bilingualism ('range of accents', 'variety of registers') in Glasgow speech. From a professional point of view they contrasted 'broad' Glasgow speech with 'Standard' or 'School' English. They differed only in how they saw the contrast occurring; more than half the teachers saw the situation as being the difference between middle-class and working-class speech. Several teachers suggested that the school situation was one where a model of Standard English was provided. In their view, middle-class children and those from 'better homes' do best in this situation because their language most closely approximates to that of the school. Similarly these teachers believe that brighter children and those from the 'better' working-class areas are most able to cope with learning the second language, School English; they learn to use a different language in the classroom from the one that they use in the home and on the playground. The not-so-bright children and those from the 'poorer' working-class areas are either not able to cope or do not want to, and tend to use the same language for speaking to the teacher as they use in their homes or on the playground.

There was total agreement that very little in the way of traditional Scots vocabulary is familiar to pupils nowadays, though they might use local 'slang':

If you read Burns nowadays, it's like reading Chaucer. When I grew up almost a third of the words were recognisable. The old Scots words which formed a fairly substantial part of Glasgow vocabulary all now need to be explained. (T23, secondary school teacher)

I have noticed a sad ignorance among students of old Scots words, for example, *thole* or *jalouse*, which are pretty widespread words, and used by past authors. (T45, training college lecturer)

Only a few informants mentioned grammar:

Grammatical structure is poor. We struggle against it without a great deal of success. It is more of a problem than accent. (T17, secondary school teacher)

My heart sinks when I get students who have satisfied the examiner in S C E, who stand up and say 'I done it', 'I seen it' – a sloppiness in language which is attributable to a mistaken social idea, that if one speaks correctly one is siding with a particular social class. This is a deplorable attitude. I tell students that they are negating whatever they have learned by this wrong-headed attitude. (T41, training college lecturer)

I don't see any difficulty with children becoming familiar with different types of speech but I think prejudice runs strongly against expressions like 'I done it' and 'I seen it'. There is the feeling that if pupils leave school habitually saying these things, then this will put prospective employers against them. (T45, training college lecturer)

So if there are 'two languages' the differences lie primarily in pronunciation, with a small number of grammatical differences. This view was supported by the university lecturer who had grown up speaking 'Glaswegian':

My recollection of it is that I can't recollect anything but pronunciation or grammatical usage, which we were told was wrong. *Mainly in the verbs*, '*I done*' *and* '*I seen*'? Yes. Simple tenses like these. It was a small number, but they were frequent in speech. You find students writing like this if that is their background. Even at high levels in English courses. (T39, university lecturer)

The other major point of concern was the ability to express oneself clearly, effectively and fluently. Most of the informants felt that there was a problem with regard to fluency, that their pupils lacked confidence in speaking and did not express themselves coherently. This opinion was found as much amongst university and training college lecturers as primary and secondary teachers, and most of the informants had something to say about it:

The children here [King's Park] are more fluent. They have a wider range of vocabulary than the children in Govan, who had a limited speech. (T22, primary school teacher)

They're unsure of themselves for a start and talking in what is almost a foreign language makes them doubly unsure. The school must do something. (T10, secondary school teacher)

96

Some working class students can't express themselves well. They find difficulty in putting words together, in making a sentence. They are very unhappy with a situation where they have been asked to speak. It's also because they have very broad Glasgow accents. (T05, lecturer)

When they said that Scottish children in general were reticent, the informants compared them with English children, and in some cases with American or Irish children:

The children in London expressed themselves far better at an earlier age, chatted a lot, and could approach adults. They were more sophisticated, more of an equal with adults. (T12, primary school teacher)

They are less fluent than pupils in England. Even where the content is originally better, the expression is better in England. There is a sort of tradition of reticence in Glasgow. It is considered not quite right to speak at length – an expression of superiority which the natives resent. (T23, secondary school teacher)

You can see this on TV interviews where you stop a group of English lads and they're all clamouring to get at the mike, whereas you go amongst a group of Scottish children – unless you pick the particular situation – and you find that they're much less inclined to speak and they speak in much shorter sentences and they're much less prepared. You might see it amongst older people, of course. I think the English system does produce a kind of articulacy on quick occasions which our system hasn't produced – until very recently, anyway. (T39, university lecturer)

The pupils here feel they're at a disadvantage. English children will make a guess at what they haven't been taught, the Scots child won't because he hasn't been taught it. The same lack of confidence applies to their speech. They feel less articulate, but I don't think it's true. (T08, secondary school teacher)

There is an inhibition in the average Scot. They are frightened of their own voices. People south of the border aren't inhibited. (T19, primary school teacher)

There is something in the temperament, something in the speech habits of the West of Scotland whereby it is not done for people to speak at any length. If you speak at length normally people won't listen. This is not so, say, for example, in the west of Ireland, where people talk and listen, and they talk at length. In the west of Scotland everybody speaks at once. They speak in short bursts. (T42, training college lecturer)

There were a few informants, however, who compared the

English children adversely with the Scots. They felt that enough had been done to encourage the children to speak up:

> We encourage them now to speak out. We weren't allowed to do it before . . . Sometimes I don't think it is a good thing. Sometimes they can sound very precocious. In England the children sound very bold. (T14, primary school teacher)

Even at the university level this difference was commented on. In response to a question whether students from England were more willing to speak in a seminar situation, one lecturer replied:

> Yes, I would say so. And partly because of their presence the others tend to be a wee bit retiring. *Why? Any answers to that one?* Because they're not bilingual in the same way. Most of the students we get from England speak the standard speech. There are some who come from the regions of England, and they're sometimes a bit hesitant in speech, but many of the students we get from England are more at home in the language. Almost any Englishman feels more at home in the language as we study it than the Scots students. (T39, university lecturer)

> One of the features of our work here in postgraduate courses is the seminars. We lay great stress on this and we do find that people with extremely good brains, who have come through the system, a remarkably high percent of them are tongue-tied, are very poor at communicating in public, whereas maybe we get a selected sample from the States or Canada, but we find that these do not have this. It may be a cultural thing, that students are reluctant to speak out because the culture doesn't encourage it. Certainly I feel that a lot of our students have done very good academic work and are just hopeless at coming in to talk in a group and often at the end of a year they're beginning to improve because it's the first time anyone has asked them to do so. *Why should this be?* Because of the educational system. For very many academic children it's still a case of sitting, listening in a class, doing a great deal of writing, similarly in university, in our own university there is a greater trend towards seminar work, and I've had students come into a seminar, take out their notebooks and expect me to talk to them for an hour. To be invited to contribute, to discuss, for some of them is a real strain and I think there is a psychological barrier here and I would attribute it mainly to the educational system in Scotland. *To the fact that they don't get the opportunity to speak?* Yes, they're not encouraged to speak as they are in other . . . certainly, America, they're encouraged far more than they are here. There's a paradox here, because in Scotland they produce some of the outstand-

ing speakers. Some of the Celts turn out to be wonderful speakers and others remain tongue-tied. (T44, university lecturer)

There were also some teachers who felt that the situation had changed or was changing, particularly in primary schools:

Nowadays the child coming to school hasn't an inhibition about coming to school as previous generations did. Children now are encouraged to express themselves, have a greater say in the set-up at home. Their opinion is asked for more than it was. (T19, primary school teacher)

There's no trouble in getting them to speak to the class. It's a matter of getting them to stop. (T21, primary school teacher)

It's changing and changing for the better. Children are more voluble and more competent at speaking. It's much better. Now, Scottish children, with the change in the curriculum are being encouraged to speak more. (T22, primary school teacher)

There has been a change in attitudes in the classroom because people have realised that language is the basis of learning and of types of learning. We are trying to get pupils to talk and to internalise their environment and to get them to organise their experience. (T30, primary school teacher)

In this school the children are more vocal and more willing to speak freely than they were in any other school. They are willing to express an opinion. (T17, secondary school teacher)

However, there were those who believe that more could be done:

There's less reticence for other reasons. They're not awed by occasions and people. They'll now express their opinions, but not with any more fluency, not expressed at any greater length . . . more willingness to express something but it's not expressed any better. (T23, secondary school teacher)

I insist to my students that they have to do a good deal more than they are doing in allowing children to speak in the classroom. One of the weaknesses in the Scottish system is that students have been taught to write and their speaking neglected. This is changing, but more could be done. A lot is being done in the lower areas of the primary school but it is not carried through. (T02, training college lecturer)

There's a tremendous difference in the amount of group activity and this sort of thing. But I don't think there is enough attention given to spoken language even at this stage [primary school] . . . There's still too much of a tendency to teach something and then make children write it down in their books. And nobody ever talks about what is going on. (T43, training college lecturer)

Few pupils have difficulties in terms of speech but there are more serious communication problems, mainly because of not enough speaking situations. In schools they're being seriously neglected in this respect. They're not encouraged to speak. (T07, secondary school teacher)

The same teacher felt that part of the problem for 'pupils who have a broad accent' is the speech and attitude of the teachers:

At all levels they resent someone whose values appear diametrically opposed to their own, that is, middle-class values: 'I'm different and I'm better and I want you to be like me.' They resent this. If you can speak as they do, you can be open with them and say that there is a better way of speaking, which is to be clearer, be aware of different modes of expression, they'll believe you and accept it. Not if you ostracise them by the way you speak. They really are self-conscious about the way they talk and they don't realise that there is anything attractive about their speech. It doesn't occur to them that they have better ways of expressing certain things than anyone else in the UK. This is because no-one tells them. You have to do this in a living way. Not by saying in a posh voice that their accent is good, but by relaxing a bit and speaking the way they do in the staff-room. There is a tendency to put on politeness which should have ended some time ago. You can get things going in the classroom by trying, although you are competing with the rest of the system, but still not on a social plane. They can speak very well eventually in classroom situations, but they still miss out on the social ones, and they feel socially inferior when they go into new situations and so they limit the number of new situations they get into. (T07, secondary school teacher)

A young primary school teacher also emphasised the value of creating the right setting for speech:

My class is willing to talk. When we hold a discussion, I don't correct the way they talk. I allow them to speak slang. There's an easy-going atmosphere, so they talk. (T29, primary school teacher)

Other teachers drew attention to resistance on the part of the pupils:

Oh yes, they'll talk to me in an easier way than they were used to. I've noticed it growing ever since I started teaching. Boys will speak in a friendlier way, but they will have reservations about speaking in their group, because of the opinion of the peer group. It's the snob thing. Your peers don't like you to speak posh. This persists till 18 or 19. (T15, secondary school teacher)

Some pupils go out to university, art school, PE college. On the whole their accent is a little better than less able pupils who take a pride in not talking posh – a deliberate resistance. (T17, secondary school teacher)

If you aim for a higher level the child will give it to you in class, but at home he will revert to the home speech. He will be ridiculed at home and he will revert. (T19, primary school teacher)

The feeling I have is that it arises from social pressures. I've had pupils who've become by dint of hard work very fluent speakers of English, in vocabulary and clarity, and could relapse into unintelligible vernacular when they were with friends and families. It arises from feeling you were acting a disloyal way if you used this type of speech. The object is to show that you aren't different. *Do pupils view that what you learn isn't relevant to real life?* I don't know that that is entirely true. They don't feel that proper speech is irrelevant. If you pushed them they would say it was superior. It is valuable, but it is suspect because they are reaching into regions which they haven't entered before and this could be, in certain circumstances, getting above yourself. They have a bit of guilt about it, that this sort of speech they should be using in an ideal world. Not a genuine contempt for the mode of speech but a general wariness about it. (T23, secondary school teacher)

We are trying to teach English, but in many cases it is a losing battle. In an area like this [Easterhouse], to speak English is regarded as cissy. (T28, primary school teacher)

The same teacher remarked that 'the teacher who insists on speaking English tends to be alien to the children' who are accustomed to 'the Glasgow tongue' of their parents. Yet he insisted that 'the teacher must speak to them in English'.

A young secondary school teacher summed up the dilemma of a new teacher:

If you talk with a cultured accent with words they don't understand, it's difficult to get across to them; if you lower yourself to their level then you don't get the respect. (T26, secondary school teacher)

Among those teachers who thought that more attention should be given to oral communication in the school there was no clear agreement about the emphasis to be given. Some were in favour of more drama and debates:

They should be given more of the speech and drama kind of thing. I give them a chance to talk on set subjects. They like it and even the quieter ones want to do it, and it's not disruptive.

They are funny and they try to be polite. *When they try to be very polite, are they good at it?* Not bad, but it's more a caricature of what they see on TV. (T31, primary school teacher)

I think that the second of the two noticeable Glasgow features, the inability to express oneself, is still the more serious and needs immediate attention. If we can get them to express themselves at greater length it can do nothing but good psychologically and academically. This is where the speech and drama teachers are helping. They are managing to break down some of the barriers. They have managed to arouse an enthusiasm for role playing. (T23, secondary school teacher)

I think there is probably quite a bit being done in schools through the debating societies. This is something that I noticed in interviewing girls hoping to come into college. Of the twenty-eight, there were some who had a lot to say. Then in asking further questions I found that most of these were members of their debating societies. This had given them self-confidence. (T40, training college lecturer)

Other teachers felt that the problem required more attention throughout the school:

People who are full of thought and can't express it are suffering. Lack of confidence in that way is a sad thing. Bottling up what you want to say, not for content but for the manner in which it is said. If you listen to the English, they are never at a loss for something to say. It is something that has to be tackled from the word 'go'. That is in every classroom situation, encouragement to speak out, to be creative must be given. *Is it an English department problem?* Every teacher is a teacher of English. In every subject there is a two-way situation and the child has got to be encouraged to give as well as take. That will change in every situation. *But people say that if you concentrate too much on this other skills will be lost?* Yes, I have said it myself, but I believe that freedom must be given unless you're going to have a tied-up individual who won't speak. (T25, secondary school teacher)

Is there a way of getting the teachers in general to encourage them to speak up? Only by a general development of methods. One would be in the school itself encouraging the teachers to adopt methods to allow this to happen, to make them aware of oral English. I agree with you. I think the danger is that in other subjects they say: 'Well you have a good time in that class standing up blethering but in our class we're going to learn something', and I think this is the difficulty that it becomes a formal lesson, and not something that is part of the entire school atmosphere. To get that in secondary school is very difficult. Much easier in primary. I think that what may happen is that because of the change in atmosphere and the emphasis of speech in primary, secondary schools will be obliged to go along with it because the children will have been socialised into communication patterns and then they will expect to be able to talk. I think there is a great danger of a conflict at the early years of the secondary because of this. (T44, university lecturer)

Other teachers saw the problem of encouraging the children to speak as one that involves the question of discipline:

We encourage them now to speak out. We weren't allowed to do it before. It helps when it is spoken rather than written. We were encouraged to write. Sometimes I don't think it is a good thing. Sometimes they can sound very precocious. In England the children sound very bold. *Does this happen in schools?* It could be worrying as far as discipline goes. (T14, primary school teacher)

This was an older teacher. A younger primary school teacher, when asked if there was a discipline problem with the freer situation, replied:

There may be more of a problem, but your outlook has to be different. You have to expect the children to talk quite freely. When you don't want them to, you have a problem to keep them quiet. (T32, primary school teacher)

This runs headlong into another problem, discipline and order.

In primary school do you feel that there is a discipline problem that interferes with the freedom that we've been talking about? I think that there were some people who always did have problems with this. Unfortunately there is a tradition in Scottish schools of people being very authoritarian and the people who believe that this is the only way to control a class are still very strong in the schools, and they tend not to appreciate the difference between a class which is less formally organised but well controlled and one which is unruly. Until we get away from this older element where people are ruled by the belt, you're always going to have certain difficulties with discipline which applies to schools. *Do you see signs of the old tradition weakening?* I would love to see it. It is weakening but it isn't going and I don't think it is going to go for a long time. I would have said until a week ago that this was pretty well on the way out when I heard a story of a teacher who had fallen off a chair strapping a child because he could hit harder that way. I would love to say that it's going, but I'm afraid it's not. I don't know how you get rid of this tradition, that if you are a disciplinarian you belt. *All the teachers I've spoken to*

103

think there is no alternative and almost all the children think there is no alternative. That is depressing. The terrible thing is that it is accepted. And I don't know what it is. Are the children here that much worse than anywhere else or are the teachers lacking in confidence in their own personalities that they don't imagine they could control children without this? (T43, training college lecturer)

Not surprisingly, the question of discipline was raised more frequently in connection with the secondary school:

I don't think I could work in a system which wasn't disciplined. There are different ways of maintaining order. I think that in this school the majority of teachers don't allow spontaneous talking in the class, because the moment they do that their authority is gone. Perhaps you should be taught to deal with that kind of situation. Most of the teachers if you walk into their class there is complete silence. Most teachers don't get silence by using the belt, but by their brand of sarcasm, or the way they speak. And yet if you go into a class where there is noise and talking other teachers will say there is no discipline. (T26, secondary school teacher)

I don't think the school situation will ever be without problems. I think that discipline, that is self-discipline, is arrived at principally through the personality of the teacher. A teacher who walks into the class and screams at the class is in grave danger of having the class scream back. A noisy teacher produces a noisy class, a dead teacher produces a dead class. The teacher who can go into a class and turn on the noise and turn off the noise is a good teacher. He can crack a joke and control the response. A class which is fully occupied is much less of a discipline problem. I've had all sorts of school experience and this is one of the things I had to learn. This is coupled with a ready wit. When a child tries it on, the teacher should have enough wit to turn the tables on big Willie without making him feel too small. (T41, training college lecturer)

I don't think that the system is really so authoritarian. I think it's an authoritarian teaching tradition, one which lays great stress on total silence in the classroom. Young teachers with noise coming from their classroom tend to be regarded as bad teachers. Sometimes it is because they are, they're not controlling their class. At other times it is simply because the good teacher is simply the one who has total silence reign. I don't really think the system is totally authoritarian in that way. I think it's . . . and even this kind of teaching may not be authoritarian . . . it's just a mode of teaching. It's a way of approaching the subject, it's a way of dealing with children,

104

which stresses silence and the absorption of information rather than the giving out. *But since the children wouldn't naturally be silent, doesn't that make it authoritarian?* Yes, I would agree with that. There is an implication of authoritarianism. Often it's a kind of benevolent paternalism where the children sit quietly and get on with their work and they're quite happy. (T44, university lecturer)

The same lecturer commented on the anxieties of the teacher:

I accept the point that the teaching is very much geared towards the written exam, that there is not sufficient encouragement of people to speak and that this has an element of authoritarianism in it. A number of people are critical of recent primary methods because children come into secondary schools and will begin asking questions without waiting till they're asked and there is this element of discipline in it which leads a number of Scottish teachers to fear speech because they say it is a breakdown of traditional discipline patterns. *Why should that fear be so great?* Because discipline is a problem. It is a much greater problem than people who have not been in schools understand. That a class which becomes unruly or impertinent can impose great strains on the teacher. A class which asks questions in a pleasant way is a delight to teach. I think a lot of teachers are afraid that if they loosen the reins of discipline and allow people to participate more, things will get out of control, children will not be quiet at the point in the lesson when they should be quiet in order to hear some really vital piece of information and I think that the question of social control and speech is something to be looked at much more closely than it has been. Because unless teachers can be persuaded that you can have communication on behalf of children verbally and still retain adequate social control then we're not going to get very far, and this is a major problem that should be looked at more closely. (T44, university lecturer)

Two training college lecturers commented on the need to instil confidence in the teachers so that they would be willing to allow their pupils more freedom:

There are many teachers who are afraid to do this. The fear is it will get out of hand. It is a real fear in the lower stream of a comprehensive with a young teacher. We can't expect that of young teachers, especially young women. I don't think much can be done in training college. This is a problem that I've worried about, but have felt despondent. (T41, training college lecturer)

The only way you can do this is to give them a good enough

105

background of knowledge so that they're reasonably confident adults and that they have a reasonable chance with their children of not being caught out. And on the few occasions when they are wrong they won't lose face by saying 'we'll have to look that one up'. You want teachers to be unafraid of allowing children to speak, to help children to refine their own ideas of language. (T43, training college lecturer)

However, it is not only a matter of background knowledge:

There's still too much of this old, traditional schoolmaster idea, or schoolmistress. There's no free and easy adult-child relationship. And you even find this with students coming into college. It's amazing how many of our first year students can't talk to a lecturer as one adult to another. *They don't get any model in the secondary school?* No, and I don't think they talk to the children in primary school as they would talk to their own families. It's a completely different idea. But I think this is terribly important. It's terrible that they've gone all the way through school and when I talk to them in the corridor they still say, 'Yes, miss'. They're not encouraged to have an adult relationship. (T43, training college lecturer)

A number of informants commented on their own anxieties in speaking:

I hated having to talk in class, though I got little of that in school. I had an oral exam on coming up to university and it was as bad as I feared. I hated tutorials when I first came to university but I soon adapted and got used to it. (T24, secondary school teacher)

If you're able to talk that is the most important thing because you have to use your mind, not your memory, as you do in exams. I personally think it's difficult to talk. It is in tutorials at university. In the three years I didn't open my mouth once in the tutorials. It wasn't that I didn't have the ideas or the knowledge, it was just having to talk in front of other people. And in university too, it's strange because a lot of them do have cultured accents which doesn't help other people a lot because their accent isn't as good. (T26, secondary school teacher)

Also I've spoken to Phil and Jeff about this and they both said that they were encouraged to speak more in an English school than we were in Scottish schools. I think this is changing a bit now. Certainly when I was in school you sat in class and listened to what the teacher said. When I came to university you knew you were supposed to speak but you were conditioned to be quiet.

I think it's an inferiority complex which a lot of Scottish

106

students have, inferior to the English students and inferior to the lecturers. It's an adolescent attitude but I know it's shared by a lot of the students – rather have a piece of paper to write on because sometimes what you're going to say isn't going to be communicated well to the lecturers. (T39, university student, prospective teacher)

I can recognise shyness in pupils because that's the way I was. I'm still frightened of public speaking although that has been bettered by experience at college and teaching. Gaining confidence is an important thing. Scots have tended not to be confident, because children have traditionally been told to be quiet. (T32, primary school teacher)

I am not as articulate as I would like to be, not as free as my children. *What was it in your background?* The type of repressive schooling. I was terrified to speak in public. *Do you think at the level of training college more could be done to help?* Yes. When we had speech training the emphasis was on correctness. But I feel that if people could talk about what they feel and what they think about, the speech would be acceptable. We've got to accept those variations in speech. Put the ability to express on expressing yourself. Twenty-five years ago I would have said that pronunciation was important. (T30, primary school teacher)

I went to school in the east end of the city. The first time I heard standard English was at school. I heard people talk about 'floors' and 'walls' which I had never heard before. It took me a while to do the translations. I enjoyed it, but it was quite difficult. We didn't expect people to speak as we did after we heard the school teachers. We knew there was some other language. There were some places which had wireless sets but we didn't have one till the war. *At what age did you begin to speak school English?* You spoke a bastard version. You tried to remember the word they would use, and they would correct us. You did grow up with a sense that what you were speaking was regarded as inferior. *When did you feel comfortable in using school English?* I think that was only when I had been teaching, because the kind of areas I moved in didn't adopt that kind of speech. Most of my hobbies were done with people who spoke basic Glaswegian. (T39, university lecturer)

This lecturer had also been away in the army and this had caused a change in his speech habits. A number of the men teachers had had similar experiences:

How did you manage to get a non-Glasgow accent? Unconscious patterning on teachers and during the war I served on

107

ships on which I was a radio officer and most of the other officers were English and this eliminated some of the Glasgow accent. (T28, primary school teacher)

During National Service I worked in Berlin. *Did your accent modify?* Yes, there were people who found Scottish speech rhythms difficult and I had to make an effort to adapt. Not so much the accent as intonation, which was the off-putting part. It's one of the things that west of Scotland speakers try first to lose. (T23, secondary school teacher)

Every person has at least two registers. I have. I can talk school patois and also hold a reasonably intelligent conversation with anyone at university. *Where did you acquire this double skill?* In the middle plus stages of my senior secondary education. At that stage I could indulge in that patois, but I'll say that for my teachers, one who said that if you persist in this you're putting yourself at a disadvantage because the big world outside of Glasgow just doesn't want to know. I took this to heart. I thought I can write correctly, why not speak correctly. But I come from a working class family and I didn't want to cause difficulty with them, putting on airs and graces, so I had to tread carefully. But coinciding with the end of my school career, began my army career and there I was put into a radar section. I was put in contact with intelligent people, university undergraduates, and they were speaking in a manner I admired, especially people from Thames valley. While I didn't ape the accent – I was speaking on RT and it was made clear to me that if I was to be understood by someone from, say, 'Brum' or Kent I would have to be able to speak clearly – from then on the habit stuck and when I went to university, I persisted with what I consider to be a clear-cut register. (T41, training college lecturer)

One young woman teacher who had grown up in Castlemilk remarked:

When I was in late secondary, I thought I was very broad and I decided to change. (T21, primary school teacher)

However, some teachers observed that pupils were often unaware of any standards by which their speech might be judged adversely:

It is only later when he leaves school and he finds his job opportunities are less that he realises how handicapped he is. (T28, primary school teacher)

Some of the speech is very slovenly. When students go out on teaching practice I think some of them become very aware for the first time that their speech is careless. I have on several occasions recorded a student teaching and they feel a bit shattered. This is a carelessness that has grown. I don't mind a Glasgow accent but I do resent careless speech, where they're clipping word endings and drawing out vowels because if the teacher is going to give this type of example, this is going to be exaggerated by the child. I expect from every student, correct speech, a good standard of speech. But as I say accent is indifferent. (T40, training college lecturer)

There were also different opinions among the teachers as to the importance of linguistic ability:

I find a lot of the children inarticulate, but it does depend on ability and character. The general level is low but it doesn't bother me because I understand what it is they want to say. Personally, I'm not convinced of the importance of the spoken word. I think there are a lot of more important skills they could be learning. You shouldn't spend too much time on it. It might be a mistake to concentrate on it. I'm probably very conservative in this. (T24, secondary school teacher)

This was the most explicit statement of this view but a number of other teachers probably shared it, to judge by their general lack of interest in the question of the effect of the pupil's ability to speak on his future prospects. Sometimes, there was almost an impression of fatalism in the response:

Most of the girls go to work in factories and there is no difficulty there. Those who want to go into an office or into university will pay attention anyway to the way they speak. People who speak badly are the ones who are going to be in factories where it doesn't matter. (T09, secondary school teacher)

Lots of employers are impressed by an easily understandable manner, but at the same time the kind of jobs that most of these pupils go for are not the kind of jobs where this would be a factor. If they did have this increased social ability they might have a wider range of jobs. (T07, secondary school teacher)

In the west of Scotland they are not likely to suffer because there isn't any social stigma attached to the way they speak. If they went further they would find that speech plays a greater part. (T23, secondary school teacher)

Other teachers thought it was important with varying degrees of emphasis:

I think that it matters probably when some of them leave schools and when they're applying for jobs, because using a very strong local speech could hinder them in certain kinds of work. (T45, training college lecturer)

There are people who still operate against folk who speak in a particular way. And it sounds very coarse. In certain circum-

109

stances it isn't a good way to communicate. It sounds very rough on the phone, it can sound harsh or callous, when it isn't so at all. If a girl is going for a job and her speech is more pleasing, she's got a better chance. *You think it really does count?* Oh, yes. I think people do operate in this way. I never want to encourage people just to be blether-skites, but if they're going to be judged at interviews on whether or not they speak, then obviously it's better that they speak. And speak fairly reasonably and coherently. If they don't then they're at a big disadvantage. (T39, university lecturer)

I would have thought it was important for everyone including the very academic too. People go for interviews for jobs. Most of the population in their daily work do not have to write very much; they're more likely to work effectively if they can communicate orally, whether it's instructing an apprentice, talking to a friend, or explaining at a meeting why they did what they did. One could argue that industrial efficiency would depend as much on oral communication as written communication. In interviews the ability to speak carries a tremendous weight. (T44, university lecturer)

I would return to my safe position and say that everyone has two registers. The gradual adoption of the more carefully enunciated register ought to be encouraged. We're mixing more and more with the big world outside. To persist in an entrenched position is very foolish as regards dialect. The only motivation is a kind of stubborness. To change it, the teachers must tread warily so as not to give offence. Point out that there are advantages in developing the second register from a purely mercenary point of view. Two people going for an interview and one speaks in the broad dialect, no matter how intelligent he is, he is going to lose out against a person who speaks correctly. It's as basic as that. At some time in school education the teacher must stand up and sell this to the student: 'You ought to try and speak in a reasonable manner, escape from the chains of your patois'. I would bring it out into the open rather than do it surreptitiously. (T41, training college lecturer)

Finally, there are a number of comments, which refer to the wider situation in the school, that impinge upon the question of speech:

I don't think you can isolate language and the use of language from the full development of the individual. And if you're not developing the individual fully in accordance with what his real nature is then anything else you do is patching up a structure that's got to crumble. (T42, training college lecturer)

Do you think the families could be brought more into the school?

110

Very much so. And I think it's an important way of doing so. And I think if we could do that, and we could, it would solve a great number of the problems for us. It might create others, but it would help us with the dreadful corporal punishment which many teachers are still obliged to use. They don't want to, they have to. I would defy a great number of people to go into the toughest areas of Glasgow and think they would survive on sheer force of personality. I would try much more to bring the community into the school to deal with these problems of social control. *The system being applied perpetuates itself. Interviewing children, the majority of them see no alternative to the belt.* That's why a young teacher walking into the school cannot overnight change it, because the children have assumptions. The whole system has assumptions. In order to change it, you've got to change the social control of the school, its community relationships, and if you get that organised you can get rid of corporal punishment. It's the only way to do it and that's why corporal punishment must be got rid of. It's ineffectual and it inhibits communication. (T44, university lecturer)

In Scotland, even today, children are considered to be a race apart and not allowed to share in what goes on. In London they had a good say and they were at ease with whoever walked in. (T12, primary school teacher)

I can remember certain members of staff who were always courteous to me as a child. These were the ones for whom we had a high regard, and those are the people you would try to emulate as a teacher. (T43, training college lecturer)

Treat them as young adults. They should do work when they're given it, but otherwise they can talk. (T32, primary school teacher)

How Teachers Described Glasgow Speech

Two sorts of description were made of Glaswegian speech, one describing aesthetic quality and the other, linguistic features. A list of the terms used to describe aesthetic quality (often modified by the phrase 'broad Glasgow speech') follows, with their numbers of occurrences in parentheses: not very nice to listen to (8), harsh (6), ugly (5), broad (5), coarse (4), rough (3), grates (3), guttural (3), slovenly (2), uncouth (1), flat (1), loud (1), nasal (1), callous (1), revolting (1), distinctive (2), homely (2), tuneful (1), attractive (1), vitality and vigour (2). There were forty-five occurrences of negative terms as opposed to eight of positive ones. However, several of the informants remarked on the way in which aesthetic considerations are affected by social considerations:

I don't find broad Glasgow accent pleasant. I just don't find it aesthetically very pleasing in some way. And it is difficult to distinguish between the aesthetic and the social in that respect. (T04, lecturer)

The distortions of Glasgow speech are so recognisable and associated with inferiority of all kinds, that you feel it is something that has to be got rid of. (T23, secondary school teacher)

A terribly broad Glasgow accent is not nice, but it is not so much the accent as what the people are saying and the way they're saying it. Very often we associate accent with drunks and women shouting. That would destroy any accent. (T18, secondary school teacher)

The terms used to describe linguistic features can be listed under four headings. a) *Pronunciation:* glottal stop (16), rolled 'r' (2), dark 'l' (2), vowels (4), dark vowels (1), 'a' (2), 'u' (1), 'i' to 'u' (1), nasalisation (2), clipping final consonants (5); b) *Vocabulary:* few traditional Scots words (20), Glasgow slang (9), Scots slang (2), valuable dialect words and phrases, which are untranslatable (2), Gaelic, Irish and Scots words (2), terse and succinct phrases (3); c) *Grammatical Structure:* variation in forms of past tense (13); and d) *Intonation:* lengthened vowels (2), stacatto rhythm (1).

Several of these linguistic features were reported as being typical of 'poor' Glasgow speech, e.g. glottal stop, dark 'l', dark vowels, Glasgow slang, variation in forms of past tense, nasalisation, lengthened vowels. Features identified positively were valuable dialect words and phrases, succinct phrases.

3. The Employers Sample

With only one exception all the informants interviewed in the employer category affirmed the importance of speaking well, particularly at the interview stage. To a certain extent this may have been exaggerated by the situation in which their opinions were solicited. The mere fact that the interview was taking place, and that the question was asked, presupposed that it was an important question. Under the circumstances, some of the informants may have felt that it was only polite to show sufficient interest in the question to avoid implying that the interviewer was wasting his time. Only one informant categorically denied the importance of speech differences:

In this context, whether a boy is articulate or not, or whether he has a peculiar mannerism, or has some physical defect, is completely beside the point. *It's totally irrelevant?* Yes. (E10, university administrator responsible for technical staff)

However, there were six informants whose responses indicated less concern with the question of speech than the majority did. On the one hand, there were the personnel managers of three factories

112

who recruited for a wide variety of jobs, in many of which speaking ability was not of paramount importance. On the other hand, the personnel managers of a national insurance company and of a firm of chartered accountants, and the assistant staff manager of a bank, also showed relatively little interest in the question, though for a very different reason. In the latter case, the lack of concern apparently followed from the little difficulty that those managers found in recruiting the personnel they needed. A somewhat similar attitude was found in two medical faculty administrators regarding applicants to the medical school because of the high competition for places. However, all the informants agreed that, other things being equal, speaking ability could be an important factor in deciding on borderline cases, but in situations where highly specific skills are required (as, for example, in a prospective chartered accountant) speaking ability is less likely to be the deciding factor.

One of the most explicit statements of the importance of speech was given by the staff manager of a marketing firm:

How many people on average are you looking for in a year? On an average year a normal intake in this particular branch would be about three to four graduates. *How many would you expect to interview to find them?* Frightening. I'm not sure of the accurate statistics, but they seem to me certainly, probably about 200 people, maybe more. *As many as that?* Yes. Our selection percentage in fact is very low, it's very low. *The selection would depend to a certain extent on the interview?* I would say it virtually depends on the interview. The other example I would give you is a person may be on paper the best qualified person in the business yet for our particular type of business really of no use at all to us. So I would say it all depends on interview.

How much attention do you pay to the way in which a person speaks? A great deal. *What kinds of things do you pay attention to?* The ability he has to express himself succinctly. The best example I can give you is I've got to imagine this prospective applicant some time in future sitting in front of the managing director of a company and possessing the ability, against the background of us giving him the correct training, to convince this managing director that he should invest in one of our systems. That is really the basic test. *What things would you mark negatively?* Well, he musn't appear nervous. If he's a bit restless in his chair and he shuffles about and he doesn't have the ability to express himself, he seems almost apologetic – these things would go against him. He has to come up to us as being very positive. I think you'd have to possess a bit of grit and determination because you know selling, people don't sit in a chair with open arms waiting to see you. So you've got to be fairly confident in your ability to persuade somebody to invest in your scheme.

   What about accent as such? Not at all, not unless it's somebody from across the waters, shall we say, from a foreign land who probably speaks broken English. But as far as the UK is concerned, no. *So someone with a very broad Glasgow accent, that wouldn't exclude him?* Provided his grammar was correct, that doesn't bother me at all. (E14, staff manager, marketing firm)

A similar point of view was expressed by the personnel manager of an engineering firm with branches in several parts of the country:

   In any interviews in which you're concerned, how much importance do you put on the way in which a person speaks? That's very important. *What do you pay attention to?* I pay attention to the way he's presenting himself. Well, you don't just look at a man as he comes in the door. Is he wearing a nice suit? Is his hair nice?, etc. He's got to be able to put himself over. I mean a person who's looking for a job has got to be able to sell himself. So when we interview people we're looking for a man selling himself. Now a man doesn't sell himself – he can sell himself by looking well – but he's got to sell himself verbally. Now having said that of course you meet the introvert, you meet the extrovert and you meet the middle-of-the-road man, although there's not many of them. You've got to sort of take the balance. For instance the introvert will be looking down all the time or he'll be looking up, he'll never look straight at you. But at the same time you've got to draw him out and ask the right question and get him to talk. You see if he can talk properly, see if he can sell himself depending on the sort of job. Communication is all important nowadays and there's no use me employing a manager at £3,000 or £3,500 a year if he can't communicate with me because if he can't communicate with me that means he can't communicate with his subordinates.

However, this informant differed from the previous one in the importance he attached to accent:

   Accent's all important. It really is. I think nowadays – one could get away with a very broad Glasgow accent, you know, when you used to talk about 'stair heeds' and stuff like that and they still do, but a man who talks like that is going to be a labourer for a long, long time, whereas the man who was brought up in a close can still talk about a close, can still talk about a 'stair head', but over the years he has developed. So I think accent is all important nowadays.

114

Let's be honest, a lot of the people who because of their accent, but who have the intelligence to be more than a bus driver, to be more than a street sweeper, to be more than a man who's serving in Alexander's store somewhere, the people like that they lack something else – they lack the drive to change their accent to get on in the world. They might have the intelligence but there's another factor missing in their make-up. But I think you're getting at: Is accent important? I think the accent is important.

For instance, if I was interviewing an accountant, and he could well be sitting in front of me with an ACMA, which is a management accounting, and he could be 28 years of age, and he could have got it by quite literally coming, dragging himself up, and he had a bad accent, and I had an ACMA who had the same ability, and a good accent, I know which one I'd employ, because I'm looking for someone who's going to grow with the job. *So it makes a difference for prospects?* I don't think that I sit and write down 'written and spoken English perfect', but it's a factor in deciding whether or not I employ a man or a woman at a reasonably senior level, but it's not particularly a factor when I'm employing a man or a woman or a boy or a girl at a low level.'

He emphasised that this was important even at the secretarial level:

It's very important, because personnel-wise, if I put a girl on the phone who has a broad Scottish accent, or a broad English accent, or whatever accent she's got, a broad Lancashire, or a Western accent – no matter where it's from – put anyone on the telephone, I think it restricts the person at the other side who's saying 'Gosh that's the personnel department. If that's the sort of standard they expect, it's not a very good firm.' So I think I would look for the more refined, local person. I'm not actually looking for an English-speaking person, but secretarial-wise I would expect a more refined local person on telephone communications. *How difficult is it to find such a person?* It's not difficult because then I'm talking about a generation of secretaries now who are probably, when they reach the stage I'm looking for a secretary the girl's probably about 28, 29 or 30. Now she's either refined herself, to use that awful expression, or she had something taught to her earlier on. (E03a, personnel manager, national engineering firm)

Most of the informants rejected the notion that accent was ever an important factor. Even the spokesman for the bank, the chartered accountants and the insurance company, who might have been expected to express concern on this point, did not feel that any kind of accent, no matter how broad, would ever be a handicap. The administrators for the medical faculty held similar views:

I would say that as far as a person's accent is concerned we don't give a damn what it is, but we're very concerned about his understanding of English and his ability to speak it and write it properly.

My own tutor group would give you an almost complete cross-section of local varieties from the fairly polished to the completely kailyard ones and it doesn't seem to make much difference at that level. (E18, senior medical faculty administrator)

However, the managing director of a local employment agency pointed out that not all employers were as tolerant as the informants' responses might suggest:

We get quite a lot of employers who specifically state that they don't want someone with a strong Glasgow accent. *You do actually get this?* Yes. *They will come out quite openly and say this?* Yes. I wouldn't employ anybody with a strong Glasgow accent in here. (E22a)

Moreover, as with the teachers, some of the employers objected to slovenly speech:

When you are interviewing someone do you pay attention to the way he speaks? What do you pay attention to? Obviously clarity of speech. You have to be able to hear what they are saying and also the way they express themselves which is very important especially for the sales assistants job because they are talking to the public. *Do you care at all about accent?* That's a difficult question. I wouldn't say regional accents but if we have someone in with a rough spoken accent then obviously I would look dubiously on that person because we look for a very good class of sales assistants. *Would you reject someone who otherwise seemed qualified, on the basis of a very broad accent?* No. If they were satisfactory in every other respect, but generally, this may not be true, but we do find that people whose accent is, I wouldn't say unacceptable, because no-one's accent is unacceptable, but you find that they are not dressed so well and are not suitable for the position anyway. (E01, staff manageress, national chain department stores)

I think communications in any business are extremely important, therefore speech and diction is of some interest. It is therefore important and I would go as far to say that a decision to engage someone or not might depend on their quality of diction as well as their verbal ability. I find that one of the drawbacks in the West of Scotland is the amount of slovenly speech, amongst young men in particular, which is a great

116

pity because a lot of them are well educated and intelligent and yet they don't do themselves justice because of this slovenly nature of their speech, indistinct diction. *Would you make this a general statement?* Yes. I think it's less noticeable on the part of graduates but then against that the graduates we see tend to be from the upper end of the upper second honours people because of the nature of the senior management training we provide. So I would say that reflects particularly even on Higher Leaving Certificate school boys. *How much importance do you attach to accent?* Not a great deal. I think it's wrong. People have different accents and we are not suggesting that everyone speaks the same or in the same manner. So, very little at all. *Because some people say that if you've gone to Fettes it's an advantage.* No. That's not the point which I hope I'm making. It's the slovenly nature of the speech and the careless speech which I'm talking about, rather than accent. (E04, personnel manager, national manufacturing firm)

For instance, if a man came in and you couldn't understand his accent for glottal stops and things like that, you couldn't understand what he was saying then we would conclude that however brilliant he was he couldn't communicate. Unless he had a job where communication wasn't important, we wouldn't consider him for it. But the fact that he had a Fife accent that was quite thick, if he had a good brain then the brain counts more than the accent. (E03b, assistant staff manager, national engineering firm)

I would say it's not so much a matter of accent but of carelessness in speech. I don't mind about accents and I don't think the world minds about accents today, but they're inarticulate, a) because they're so careless in the way they speak and b) they don't wish to communicate. I'm sure this is true. (E12, senior administrator, Centre for Secretarial Studies)

Several employers emphasised the value of having a local accent for communicating with customers:

How much attention do you pay to the way in which a person speaks? Well obviously that's the first thing that hits you – it's how a person speaks. But one must be consciously aware of the fact that you mustn't be too influenced by that. Again of course it depends on the job because someone who's going to be a car salesman I'd want him to be a better speaker or able to present his case or talk more easily than I would, say, a service manager.

Does that include things like accent? No, not so much accent as being able to speak freely and easily without stumbling and

117

using too many words in the wrong way. This sort of thing. *Would any accent ever exclude someone?* Why should we only consider the bad aspects of a broad accent? There's something also terribly wrong if someone came in here with a 'terribly terribly' accent; it wouldn't necessarily fill the bill either. *They could be inappropriate either end?* Yes, exactly. *So a public school accent wouldn't be an asset necessarily?* No, it wouldn't necessarily be an asset, no. Quite frankly I have a rather strong little thing about this, that if someone wanted to be a salesman for instance – and this is where you tend to get the type of public school boy who hasn't quite made the career in some of the other avenues of career development in life – a number of them tend to come back to car selling with some of the bigger companies, and they're not always the type because people don't want to think they're being talked down to or feel terribly inferior to the person who's trying to sell them something. They like to think they could be on equal even-steven terms with them.

What about the other end of the scale? Yes, at the other end of the scale I think you have to be very careful too. A man would need to have some terribly good attributes which would be easily spotted, recognised and accepted by somebody who was speaking to him and if this was so I'd be prepared to accept somebody with a very broad accent – in fact I have done this. I had one particular man who was one of our very successful salesmen recruited from the workshops. He'd been an apprentice mechanic, gone through all the workshop background but wanted to be a salesman so we gave him his opportunity. His worst fault was the way he spoke, but he is an excellent salesman, most popular with many, many customers, and he's now in fact head of a department. *Did he change the way he spoke at all?* No, not at all and he himself was always very conscious of it and quite confidentially often asked if there was anything he could do, any specific classes or anything that he could do for himself to improve this thing that he considered to be a bit of a drawback. *So he considered it more of a drawback than it proved to be?* Exactly, yes. *He was quite effective?* Yes, very effective. In fact, if I could enlarge on that, he is in fact our Used Vehicle Manager today. Now of course, in that particular job it's not so terribly important to be as grammatically correct or to speak with an accent as it might be with some of the other sales managers on the New Cars because he's dealing with a different type of client although that gets better and better all the time too. But he's also dealing with traders and he's dealing with an entirely

118

different group of people most of the time, and it's not so important. (E20, managing director, car distributors)

There was agreement among those employers who were concerned about speaking ability that the crucial point was during the initial interview, since it is then that many candidates are eliminated:

At an interview stage, where somebody's not one of your team and you've got the choice of taking them or not taking them at that stage it's critical – qualifications are critical at that stage. All sorts of other things are critical. Having got the person into the company there's a completely different set of rules once you've got in, a completely different set of rules. Somebody may be taken aside and it's mentioned to him, 'Look, you're in trouble because people don't like the way you speak.' I've never heard of it, but it's possible that that might happen. Thereafter, it depends on your performance, but at the stage where you've got the option of taking somebody or not taking somebody then it does play a very big part. (E08a, staff manager, engineering firm)

The interview is particularly crucial for the young school-leaver:

If you stop to think what are you looking for in an interview, you're looking to see whether the person is motivated. It's the most difficult interview situation of them all, for he as a school-leaver has no past experience, successes, failures, other than those which are purely academic which are not necessarily of tremendous interest to you, they have a passing interest. So, what you're trying to do then is to find out whether this chap is keen to take up a career in engineering and if he can't express it, then he's doomed and unfortunately this is one area where I think we are abysmally bad with that type of youngster who's coming out to become a craftsman or even a semi-skilled person. (E02, staff manager, national engineering firm)

I'm positive that there are sixteen- or seventeen-year-old boys coming in here who, had they been brought up in a different area, if they'd lost their fathers and mothers at the age of five and gone to live with an aunt they'd have done far better for themselves because the aunt was a cultured individual who realised the importance of language and I'm sure we turned down boy after boy because of his inability to tell us of his feelings, what motivates him, what he wants to do, what he thought about his parents, what he thought about his headmaster. It's inside him, but he doesn't know how to express it, and we have no way of getting it out, so we perhaps cut off budding brilliant engineers in their prime simply because they haven't the ability to recognise what's inside them.

Well, let's be quite clear, you can give a boy or anybody all the tests you like but in the long run it's subjective judgement that usually decides whether a man gets employment or not, and I hope that we'll never get so objective that it's a test that decides whether you get employed or not. *There are a lot of things that enter into subjective judgement?* Oh, there are appearance, the length of his hair, whether he's got a squint, whether he picks his nose, whether he hesitates and says 'ah' every other word, whether he can run a couple of sentences together, whether he uses the wrong word in the wrong context, and so on – there are so many – and language and communication is a great big part of it. (E03b, assistant staff manager, national engineering firm)

I think it's fair to say that we do make a distinction between those who are able to communicate and those who aren't. There is a large proportion of these that we discount because of that. They might be interested, they might be bright, but they're so unable to communicate to people that we just don't think of them. (E08b, assistant staff manager, engineering firm)

How much attention do you pay to the ability of an apprentice to express himself? Well, we do really take this into account quite a lot because we have a panel of people interviewing them with myself on the panel, the training officer and the manager of the particular office they're going to, and obviously this is important – if the boy doesn't come over well he makes a bad impression on everyone. I don't altogether blame the boys; I sometimes feel that when they're faced with a panel of people it's really rather off-putting, but I think that at the same time the boy who expresses himself well, providing that he has done equally well in the examinations, is the boy who has a better chance of getting a job. *Would you say that most of them can express themselves fairly well?* Not really. *Although this may not be an important factor for them at school, it may be when they come up for interview?* Well, I think it's very important because obviously if we're taking young men on as apprentices the young men we take on now are boys that we hope will be able to be promoted in later years and if they don't come over well at the interview initially, naturally it does put the interviewers off a little. (E07, staff manageress, local factory)

Several informants commented on the unsatisfactory performance of school-leavers in the interview situation:

I think everybody finds this in the industry. They are very badly prepared for an interview. They find it very difficult to express themselves. We find fifteen- and sixteen-year-olds

120

have no idea how to conduct themselves for an interview. They answer the question with 'yes' and 'no' without making any further comment and are quite prepared to sit and let you talk. You really have to work at bringing them out. They are not prepared to make any effort themselves. They have no idea what to expect. (E01, staff manageress, national chain of department stores)

There's absolutely no relationship between the academic qualifications a candidate has and his use of the language. Certainly there's no relationship between the Highers and O's he's got and his articulate use of the language. Our biggest problem is getting them to speak at all in the interview situation and I think that would go right across the academic scale and age scale. *So it's fairly general?* Yes, it's fairly general I would think. Girls, I would venture to suggest and no more, are a bit more loquacious than the boys. They have a more natural patter, the viva voce thing that comes a little bit more to life and a boy seems more fond of the grunty, monosyllabic type of answer. 'Do you really want a job of work with the Corporation, Willie?' 'Uh-huh', is the answer. 'If the Provost said to you, Willie, that you could sack anyone here and get his job what poor soul is going out on the streets and the snow?' Well, you can record a long pause, and 'I really don't know', 'It doesnae matter'. The boys I think are slightly more monosyllabic when you drag a reply out of them. (E15a, establishments officer, Glasgow Corporation)

His colleague emphasised the importance of performance in the interview situation:

So far as the use of the language is concerned in the interviewing situation – most of our appointments in departments would be done on the basis of an application form and a face to face interview – we can really only assess the acceptability of a person generally by information we have and what he or she is prepared to tell us and consequently in that situation you're depending on his ability to communicate. I don't think we would write a person off in any situation either because he speaks with an accent – frightfully decent, or be it very broad – but we really just couldn't get anywhere with anyone who just wouldn't speak and so it is very important I would have thought in that situation.

In the situation in Glasgow just now, anyone who's looking for clerical assistants we can give them ten application forms for every single appointment that they want to make. Most of the youngsters will have come from roughly the same background, roughly the same educational ability and what have

121

you, and consequently in the interviewing situation, why should the interviewer spend a lot of time trying to drag out of the mumbler the information when he's got another half dozen who will serve his purpose equally well? *This can be crucial to the youngster at the interview stage although he might not realise it?* It's crucial to the youngster, it's in no way a prejudice or anything else on the part of the interviewer. (E15b, establishments officer, Glasgow Corporation)

A number of informants remarked on the reluctance of candidates for a job to ask questions:

They must initiate relevant points in the conversation. If it's a one-way conversation from me to him, then it's a complete waste of time. Ideally people should have given —— some thought before they came to them, they should ideally, again, be thinking in terms of a career with —— . If they haven't thought of these terms then we're wasting both our times, I think (E14, staff manager, marketing firm)

Well, many of them are very nervous because they think they're up for a grilling. They don't understand it's to be a two-way exchange and that we want them to ask questions. So sometimes we feel that perhaps they're not prepared with questions – they haven't thought that this would be an opportunity for them to ask questions and when we ask them at the end, 'Now have you any questions?', quite a lot of them are struck dumb – they haven't thought – and perhaps when they've gone away they might write in and say, 'Well I should really have asked you this when I was up'. (E13, administrative assistant to medical faculty)

Not many of them ask questions? Not terribly many, other than simply to respond to an invitation, 'Is there anything you'd like to ask us?'; they say, 'If it says three weeks on the form, does that mean I get three weeks' holiday?' – you know, totally artificial. (E15a, establishments officer, Glasgow Corporation)

Even those who were concerned with the recruitment of graduates were not always satisfied with the candidates' performance:

There was one chap I'd loved to have taken, he was a very high-powered mathematical man, but I just could not get this chap to talk – 'Yes', 'No', 'I don't know.' 'Why have you come to see me? What attracts you to insurance?' 'I don't know.' 'Did the Appointments Officer tell you?' 'Yes' – and he came from a very humble stock, his father was a fisherman and his other brother was at the university, and I thought two brothers at university from a fisherman, admittedly he's probably raking in £100 a week on the fishing, but I just felt

122

this boy wants a chance, but what could you do, you could get nothing out of him. 'Where would you like to work?' 'I don't know.' (E09, personnel manager, national insurance company) The real reason for recruiting at university stage is to try and restock the management side of it. We know that the person is relatively proficient because they've got through a university course. We're not too worried about the degrees that are coming out at the end of it – what we are worried about is the ability to deal with people, and a great part of that is their ability to communicate, So what we're really recruiting is a mature, fairly well balanced, articulate person. *When you interview them do you pay attention to their language?* Up until now I hadn't separated that as being something that one does. One would write down, 'well spoken, reasonably well dressed, neat, attentive, interested, alert', these sorts of words.

Do you ever write down a negative of 'well spoken'? Very often I'm putting down a negative. *On what basis?* You would be putting down things like, 'unable to get his ideas over'; you would put down something like – I'm trying to think of certain people where I've actually done something like that – you would put down things like 'inarticulate', I would use that sort of word and that would mean to me that the person was slipping and stammering and hadn't very much to say, or you put down that he merely answered each question with a 'no' or a 'yes', he was unable to think of taking the question which was really only something to open him up. *What percentage would you say come into this category of negative comments about their speech?* Well I talked to about eighty this year and of the eighty – if you're taking the ones that were negative for that reason – it probably was about fifteen, but if I were to say the other way round the ones that I was particularly interested in because they were able to communicate I would say about only twelve. One of the worst years I've ever come across.

I'm surprised we have such a small choice from such a large number available. We get large hosts of people in each category coming forward, we manage to get the numbers we happen to need, but it's a disproportionate number compared with the overall number. The number of graduates this year that I would have taken was twelve out of eighty. We wanted fifteen people for different jobs – we had them all worked out beforehand – and it was left to me to say 'I didn't think the quality was there', I didn't have to go for them so I didn't. I said, 'Right, we're short this year.' Then we looked down to England and went to various universities in England and sent out information and tried to do a sell down there because we just couldn't find enough. I brought an American, he's over just now on a year's exchange visit, he's a personnel manager from America, and he's also shocked at the lack of confidence, the lack of bite, that people just had nothing to sell, they were just sitting there and you'd say, 'Well now, have you been interested in engineering all your life?' 'Yes.' 'What form did this take?' 'Well I'm not sure about that.' 'Did you ever have a motorbike or something? What brought you into this?' 'No, no, my uncle's an engineer.'

They're just negative characters the whole time partly because, I don't know if it's confidence rather than speech or not. *So that the eighty on paper, they were all equally qualified?* Yes, they were all equally qualified, but we couldn't find fifteen that would suit us. (E08a, staff manager, engineering firm)

We were terribly impressed with the people we saw from Aberdeen, Inverness and around that area. Not just at Aberdeen but the ones we saw at Glasgow and Edinburgh who were from that area. They were very good this year, in fact the first four people that we selected and we only selected eight in total are all from around about Aberdeen, Buchan, around that area. Incredibly. But it's happened that half our intake has come from there and a lot of that has been due to two things. One, the ability to express, and two, the personality that comes through from that, the sort of relaxed ability to express as well. *Could you elaborate now on the negative side of the candidates locally whom you did not prefer over the others?* Yes, I could almost say and this is a word I hate using, but if I was asked to say what was the difference between the candidates in the way they talked to us, there was a sparkle in one group and in the use of language that there wasn't in the other. I think perhaps that we Glasgow people tend to be a bit dull in the use of language. (E02, staff manager, national engineering firm)

Quite a few informants made 'odious comparisons', either unsolicited or in response to specific questions:

I think this is something that is lacking in Scottish people in general. I don't know whether it's a lack of confidence. They don't generally express themselves terribly well. If they're good they're very good. I find English people, people coming from abroad, can express themselves very well. But in Scotland they don't seem to – maybe it's just our dour natures, I don't quite know. Could be something to do with that. (E07, staff manageress, local factory)

I think generally speaking people from down south communicate far better than people from the west of Scotland. A person from the west of Scotland has got an inbuilt shyness, which a lot of people don't recognise. A Scot in himself has got, I think, an inbuilt shyness, and I think that this sometimes inhibits him from putting himself over properly. So therefore a man from London and a man from the Midlands or somewhere like that, forgetting about the accent, will probably put himself over better initially. (E03a, personnel manager, national engineering firm)

I think it goes beyond just necessarily our narrow interview situation. I travel on the bus for example and you overhear a lot of non-conversation which again is quite monosyllabic or there's a chatterer and the rest just interpolate the odd comment. One is a confirmed gas bag and there's a sort of grunty 'och aye, och no' thing round about. Not the same as one hears sitting in a London tube for example. This is a) Scottish and b) west of Scotland and Glasgowy. You get the, 'He talks too bloody much, a nice fella – he talks too much.' It's in a way regarded as a kind of fault, not a complete black mark, but you're slightly suspicious of it – 'He's a con man', this 'gift of the gab' thing often in a derogatory sense.

One of the things that I always feel a little cheered up about is when I hear some of the students at our universities interviewed on television and hear how inarticulate so many of them are, I get quite cheered by the four O-level types we get here sometimes.

So it isn't just at that level? I think in an adult context too at these dreadful seminars, conferences and things that my colleague here keeps encouraging people to go off on, if they're within Scotland the question time is usually a great void; if it's south of the border the questions are asked by English people until it's almost time to stop and then the Scot present picks up enough courage to ask probably the most sensible question of the session but it's just before the bell for tea. One of the difficulties I think of chairmanning such meetings in Scotland is to gauge the amount of time that they're going to leave between saying, 'Anyone got any questions?' and the wrap up, thanking various speakers profusely for their intelligent and ingenious and inspiring and interesting statements and comments and what not. That again I think is a reflection of this inarticulateness-cum-shyness that seems to divide.

It's not a lack of knowledge? You know, two hours later in a nearby pub, those fellows may well be talking their heads off till long past closing time. I don't necessarily suggest that it's the alcoholic influence, but the change of atmosphere and not being across a room, across a table, whatever, a 'we' and 'they' situation. They can gas away for hours. (E15a, b, establishment officers, Glasgow Corporation)

There is a clear shyness or reserved nature on the part of the western Scot probably in the east of Scotland but I think more so in the west of Scotland. They feel out of place, they are no less intelligent than anyone else but they certainly don't appear to have the same confidence in speaking and they don't have the same degree of maturity it would appear at interviews, like in comparison with their counterparts in England and also from some other parts of Scotland, with one exception those who have attended either public schools or boarding schools because they stand apart for this very reason that they have obviously included in their curriculum or training some aspect of debating because they have a clear advantage. It's quite obvious at interviews. *You mean fee-paying schools?* Yes. If you talk about some of the Edinburgh schools or Glasgow Academy and Gordonstoun you see boys from there and these boys are much more confident and mature in manner than the boys from corporation schools.

This problem seems to be confined to the west of Scotland. Your point about accents leads me to wonder, and I've often thought about it, that even places like Northern Ireland where they have a very strong accent, the quality of their speech and their confidence is more akin to the English general pattern and they don't have the same degree of slovenly speech or bad grammar. I think also the north of Scotland is similar to that. They don't have the same problem in Aberdeenshire and round these areas, and Edinburgh to some extent also it's not as marked. It seems to be confined to the west of Scotland and certainly to Lanarkshire which must be about the worst area. Ayrshire also to some extent. It's a lack, I think, of self-expression also. They're certainly a lot more reserved with people, even the tough nuts amongst them are quite reserved when you talk to them. And a lack of confidence. As I said, I'm not referring to intelligence because I don't think that's true, I think it's just a lack of confidence. In some ways it's often appeared to me to be an inferiority complex. (E04, personnel manager, national manufacturing firm)

This personnel manager also commented on the effect of a period away from Glasgow on young employees:

This is the head office of a number of companies throughout the UK and it has occurred that most of the young men who join our commercial apprenticeship scheme have to spend a fair part of their training period away from Glasgow in

126

various parts of the UK and the difference in maturity, ability to speak, is marked after a year or two years away from here, away from the west of Scotland. So they obviously take note. *It's not individual capacity then?* No, it's the environment really. It's certainly not the capacity. So that whilst some of them never change, the vast majority, and even the parents have remarked the difference when they come back after a year or a couple of years. It makes a difference. I don't mean they lose their Scots accent. That's not the case, and I hope that they wouldn't. But they are more confident, more mature generally and the quality of their speech is better. *Quality in what sense?* Well, the slovenliness is dropped and they think a bit more before they speak. Obviously they've had difficulty in being understood by other people. (F04, personnel manager)

Other employers commented on the advantages of attending a fee-paying school:

They seem to conduct themselves that bit better and they seem to have more assurance in themselves and confidence seems to be brought out much more in them.

After apprenticeship we sponsor certain boys to go to university to take a degree. Now each year five, six boys will come forward. Two of them perhaps have been to Glasgow Academy, four of them have left at fifteen and come through the other way. At that stage it becomes very noticeable that two of them are polished, able to handle themselves. It may be education, it may be their family life or background is such that they're used to this, they can conduct themselves, they know what we're looking for; the other chaps find it a very embarrassing thing to come forward and talk about what they're wanting to do. At that stage it's very noticeable and we're then talking about how quickly they could perhaps go into sales. Now you think twice about considering the other ones to put them in immediate customer contact, whereas their ability is exactly the same. (E08a, staff manager, engineering firm)

Yes, quite definitely I think there is. I've had salesmen and professional accountants and so on, and you can see quite a decided difference. The fellows who've been to a fee-paying school have greater confidence, they can express themselves in a better way, they don't have affected accents always, you can still speak very nicely and plainly and simply, but they're very lucid and can express themselves with greater freedom. Overall their speech is vastly superior. (E20, managing director, car distributors)

The majority of the employers were sympathetic about the

127

problems of the schools and not disposed to be too critical of the educational system or the teachers. There were, however, a number of negative comments:

I would say the west of Scotland education system is not tremendously successful at the lower end in terms of age. It improves later on. There are some areas where they're remarkably good. If we want a west of Scotland generalisation, they're not bad when they come out of the secondary at the end of their secondary course, but when they're coming out at fifteen and sixteen I think we've got troubles there. (E02, staff manager, national engineering firm)

My basic experience has come from interviewing these kids coming out of school and I don't think they're prepared in any way, shape or form for coming out of school. They don't seem to be taught or trained in their last six months as workers, they're still schoolchildren and there's nothing being emphasised to them on how they should attend an interview and that kind of thing. They're not prepared in any way. (E22b, assistant manageress, employment agency)

I think that the first thing that the schools have got to do is to do a far better job of guiding the people in their careers advisory service. Too many people come into an industry because their father was in it, or because their uncle knows somebody who'll give them a job, rather than coming into an industry because they have been convinced by logical argument, by the careers master that your skills, your strengths will make you better fitted to be A, B, C or D, and I think that would be a great contribution if the schools could say: 'This man has got skills with his hands. I think he could make a craft apprentice.' And what I'm really saying is that schools and industry have to get much closer together so that industry can communicate to the schools to give them an indication of what input they will require in the years to come, to give the schools their opportunity to produce that output to meet the industry's requirements. (E03b, assistant staff manager, national engineering firm)

I think the school's job, well, from our interview point of view, is to supply them with sufficient information so that they'll be able to ask relevant questions when they come up. This is really a different question from what you're asking but it is relevant from our point of view. Often they ask us the silliest questions which a little bit of background work by the careers department perhaps in the school would have been able to clear out of the way. We sometimes wonder how they even arrived at the idea of applying for medicine because their

128

information seems so limited. (E13, administrative assistant to medical faculty)

I don't think it [inarticulateness] really matters very much. I would think that generally speaking when they overcome the original shyness, they speak up anyway. It's a natural nervousness which you get at interview if you're sufficiently interested. I think the way in which the school could contribute a lot more would be in trying to give more positive and clear guidance, trying to sort out – of course one of the problems is that school teachers don't know very much about what jobs are available, they tend to go straight from college to schools without really seeing anything else – but I think this is the most positive thing that they could do, the teacher must know the pupil better probably than anyone including the parents in many respects, in respect of their capabilities, and should be able to guide the individual pupil towards the sort of job that would suit him best and should ideally be able to tell them where to go and how to go about getting that sort of a job. This would be very helpful. It would perhaps save us from making some mistakes.

As it is, you have to go on the interview? Yes, and one of the big problems is that the children very often haven't been told what life in the factory's like, what life working in a shop is like, you have to try and see what their ideas of work are and see how well they would fit in with a factory job. Quite frequently I've told children that they should go and look for office jobs or that they should go along to Lewis's or Marks and Spencer's to see if they can get a job there because it would appear that their ideas of work seem to coincide with office work than with operators. Career guidance doesn't seem to do very much as far as I can gather, in Scottish schools. (E19, staff manager, local factory)

Two employers commented adversely on the raising of the school leaving age:

I think I could make some valid criticisms about the lower end of the scale. We're getting now people coming in with a fistful of, not dollars, but O-levels that to our generation are meaningless and if I facetiously say that they give away certain O-levels for sweeties I don't think we're so far wrong. But there again if I can get young people coming in here with three Highers, they may have a couple of A grades and maybe eight O-grades, then we're interested. So I would say that at the lower end of the scale, we're getting people coming forward that are no better educated than they were at the end of our fifteen-year-old education, but they're coming with these certificates which the kids feel is something and in all honesty to us as the buyers are not really worth very much. (E08a, staff manager, engineering firm)

Not very happy about it at all, as a matter of fact. Well, I feel that over the years instead of the educational system supposedly improving, that in fact the standard of young person coming out of school today is considerably lower. *So you find a deterioration?* Very much so. *Over how long in terms of deterioration?* I would say possibly that I have noticed this creeping in since they raised the school leaving age to fifteen, gradually since then I would say. I would say that the young person who left school at fourteen years of age up to that point she was learning something in the school all the time and she was paying attention to what was being taught. The child who has no intention of going any further when they increased the leaving age, the extra year at school was so much wasted time; they got into lax habits, I think and I don't think this has ever changed really. *So with the school leaving age going up to sixteen?* I shudder. (E07, staff manageress, local factory)

Finally, a comment from an outsider:

Well, let's take speech. I'm an English person and I probably stand to be shot down in flames but I feel that the standard of education for O-levels and A-levels in England is higher than O-levels and Highers in Scotland. Now people that I speak to disagree entirely with this. I feel that the standard of education in Scotland on the English side is not high enough. *In what ways could it be improved?* I think very much on the subject you're interested in and that's speech, being able to make sentences, being able to convert thoughts into sentences quickly. I find that if anybody, be they Glasgow, Edinburgh or Timbuctoo, if they have time to make up a sentence in their own mind before answering a question then it usually comes out reasonably well, but in straightforward conversation between two people, between myself and a strong Glasgow person, I find that there's an awful lot of bad English comes back. (E22a, managing director, employment agency)

9. Educational Implications

> Well, I maintain that children basically aren't stupid. It's just, how much interest have they got?
>
> 047, class IIb woman

THE EVIDENCE PRESENTED in the preceding chapters raises important questions regarding the educational policy in Glasgow Corporation schools. As was shown in chapter 4 there are differences in pronunciation that correspond to differences in social class as determined on an occupational scale. In chapter 7 it was demonstrated that Glaswegians can make consistent judgements about their fellow-citizens on the basis of short samples of recorded speech. In chapter 8 it was made clear that quality of speech is often an important factor in success in higher education and employment. Moreover, many employers felt that applicants from outside the West of Scotland or from private schools were likely to be more articulate and more confident in speaking up than those who had been educated in Corporation schools. It is possible that the evidence collected in these chapters is misleading or even erroneous, but if it is not, then there is a clear case for examining the situation carefully to see whether any changes in educational policy would be advisable. It must be emphasised, however, that the following discussion is based on the comments made by pupils, parents, teachers and employers. It is not based on an examination of what actually happens inside the school or inside the classroom. The accuracy of the criticisms and the extent to which any changes are feasible or desirable must be decided by those who are directly involved in the educational system. As stated in the introduction, the intent of the present report is not to dictate to anyone what ought to be done but rather to draw attention to the issues in the hope that they will receive the serious consideration that, to an outside investigator, they seem to deserve.

The first area of concern is pronunciation. It is clear from the remarks quoted in chapter 8 that there is great confusion regarding 'accent', and the reasons are not hard to discover. On the one hand, accent is seen as providing local identification as regards both nationality and citizenship. In this respect, Glaswegians are proud of their accent, in much the same ways and with many of the same conflicting emotions, as they are of their city. On the other hand, it is clear that some Glasgow accents are less acceptable socially and in certain spheres of employment than others. Since Glaswegians do not think of themselves as snobbish, for the most part, there was some embarrassment for the informants in discussing the question of social judgements of accent. Among the teachers particularly there was often strong resistance to the suggestion that accent might be important, and many of them would no doubt have agreed with one of their colleagues:

> Exhibiting good manners is more important than accent. What we like here is a code of behaviour, which is what they lack and what disadvantages them. If you're going to get a job on the basis of accent, then we need another law against discrimination. (T08)

In general, the teachers in primary and secondary schools showed a very tolerant and enlightened attitude towards their pupils' accents. In principle, this would appear to be an asset in the school system and one that would help to give the pupils confidence in their own form of speech. Yet the evidence of some of the informants about their own feelings of insecurity, and the comments of employers, university lecturers and training college lecturers show that the main criticism of school-leavers is their lack of confidence in speaking. This paradox needs careful examination.

1. It is possible that the situation is changing and perhaps it is merely a matter of time before the full effects are felt. Certainly, there is some evidence for this in the comments of teachers and employers. However, most of the evidence suggests that the situation has not changed very much and that the majority of school-leavers are insufficiently at ease in adult conversations.

2. There are some indications that teachers are not always as sympathetic, in practice, towards their pupils' accents as they may claim to be. The number of comments on 'slovenly speech' are evidence of this. It is also possible that the teachers interviewed were not representative in their attitudes towards their pupils' accents.

3. There is the implicit criticism of the pupils' accents in the teacher's own form of speech. Teachers are usually careful to speak 'correctly' in class and are anxious to avoid 'coming down to the level' of some of their pupils.[1] While it is obvious why teachers wish to do this, the result, as one teacher pointed out, may be 'to ostracise the pupils by the way you speak'. The alternative, he suggested, was to make it clear to the pupils that their own speech is valuable and attractive. But, he went on, 'You have to do this in a living way.

---

[1] Ballantyne (1973, 36) in his survey of the attitudes of Glasgow school-children quotes the following remark by a pupil: 'It is boring because Mr —— speaks so polite and he speaks with his teeth together and you can't understand a word he says.' Cf. Creber (1972, 111): 'In the past for many, both teacher and taught, the classroom has been a total inhibitor of the natural voice.'

Not by saying in a posh voice that their accent is good but by relaxing a bit and speaking the way you do in the staff-room' (T07). So the pupils may be made to feel that their speech is inferior even though the teacher does not say so explicitly.

4. There is the notion of the 'two-language' situation, in which working-class pupils, particularly, are believed to speak one language, 'English', in the classroom and another language, 'Glaswegian', elsewhere. It is clear that this is an unsatisfactory view of the situation. It is not true that a large number of working-class Glaswegians speak two 'languages' under any reasonable definition of 'a language', although it is certainly the case that many of them may change their style of speech according to the situation in which they are speaking. However, these stylistic changes are mainly in pronunciation, with a few grammatical differences and a small number of lexical differences, mainly expressions that are often referred to as 'slang'. Although the present survey, because of the way in which the data were collected, cannot provide adequate evidence on this point, there are no indications of a 'Glasgow dialect' distinct from other forms of English, as, for example, the Buchan dialect in north-east Scotland. Instead, there is in Glasgow a wide range of varieties of English, differing mainly in pronunciation. However, as will be suggested below, the prevalence of a belief among teachers in a 'two-language' situation may have had unfortunate consequences in the school.[1]

5. There may be many teachers who are unconcerned about the way their pupils speak from one of two reasons: 'It doesn't bother me because I understand what it is they want to say' (T24); 'In the west of Scotland, they are not likely to suffer because there isn't any social stigma attached to the way they speak' (T23). As is apparent from the comments of employers in chapter 8, teachers who are unconcerned about their pupils' use of language may be leaving those pupils at a disadvantage in seeking employment.

The whole question of pronunciation or accent is a tricky and highly emotional one. Individuals do not change the way they speak lightly or without adequate reason, and there would be nothing more absurd than the attempt to promulgate unrealistic standards of pronunciation in the schools. Yet, there is nothing to be gained by pretending the problem will go away if nobody looks at it. If it is the case that a fairly large number of working-class pupils are likely to be judged adversely on their speech when looking for a job, perhaps the schools should bring the problem out into the open and make sure that pupils are aware of the criteria by which they may be judged. At present, it would appear to be a

[1] See Sledd (1972) for a criticism of the notion of biloquialism (i.e. a 'two language' policy) in the United States.

matter of luck or family background whether any pupil in a Corporation school receives any advice on his or her speech.

However, it is generally agreed that the matter of accent is, or should be, trivial in terms of the assessment of an individual's capabilities and it is probably true that most employers in Glasgow are not greatly concerned about accent. Nevertheless, it is highly likely that accent is an important factor in what most people consider a more serious problem, inarticulateness. Although not all informants saw it as a problem there was widespread agreement that many young Glaswegians are often inarticulate, tongue-tied, lacking in fluency and incapable of expressing themselves clearly and effectively. Some informants considered this a characteristic trait among west of Scotland people, almost an inherited disposition. Yet it can hardly be that, since, in general, middle-class pupils were rated superior in this respect to working-class pupils, pupils at fee-paying schools superior to those at Corporation schools, and graduates above non-graduates. More significant still are perhaps those informants who commented on the improvement in speech that followed an extended absence from Glasgow at a crucial age. If it is not inherited, what is it that makes the young Glaswegian inhibited about speaking?

The common thread that runs through the comments of informants on their own speech and that of their pupils or of their employees is the question of confidence. Again and again, informants commented on shyness, feelings of inferiority and lack of confidence. Moreover, these comments were not restricted to any single age-group or social class. Young school-leavers were reported to gain confidence after some time in regular employment, undergraduates between matriculation and graduation, junior executives during their training periods, and teachers during their first year of teaching. Much of this is the natural result of developing skills and widening experience. Yet the notion persists, among some of the lecturers and some of the employers, that the schools are not providing their pupils with the best preparation for entering the adult world of employment. If it is true that the fee-paying schools are succeeding better than the Corporation schools in this respect then it is a cause for concern, although, obviously, the two kinds of school differ also in the range of family backgrounds among their pupils. It may simply be the case that those who have attended fee-paying schools are more confident and articulate because of the kind of homes in which they have grown up.

However, it is also possible that those with the greatest advantages at home with regard to speech also receive the most favourable treatment at school. Looking at it from the other side, it is unfortun-

134

ate, to say the least, if the schools do not succeed in helping those who have the greatest disadvantages at home with regard to speech. If it should turn out to be the case, which is in no way proven, that the schools do best with those who have least need and do worst with those who have most need, then it would be true, as one employer remarked, that the rich are getting richer while the poor stay poor, at least in this respect. The question that then arises is: Are there any conditions in the schools that possibly contribute to the inarticulateness of their pupils? In attempting to answer that question it is necessary to reiterate that the following points are based on comments by informants and not on observations of what goes on in the classroom.

1. There is the traditional emphasis on writing in Scottish schools. Although there have been many changes in the primary school, particularly in the infant school, there is apparently still a strong emphasis on written work in the secondary school. There are many reasons why this emphasis should remain, but while it does it is perhaps hardly surprising that less attention is paid to speech. Since both writing and speaking are manifestations of linguistic competence, there is no conflict in developing both skills equally but, in practice, the emphasis on writing in the schools at present seems to be at the expense of speaking ability.

2. There is the role played by examinations. Because almost all examinations are written and because success in higher education depends on passing written examinations, the principal aim of the schools is to prepare their pupils for such examinations. As a result, school work that is not directed towards examinations tends to be treated as less important both by teachers and by pupils. Because nobody takes an official examination in speaking, there is little motivation for teachers or pupils to pay attention to speech. However, in the interview situation school-leavers are, in fact, often subjected to the equivalent of an oral examination. Unfortunately, the results are usually not made public and there is little feedback to the school system.

3. There is the question of class size. It is obviously harder to allow freedom to speak in a class of forty than in one of, say, ten. Many classes in Corporation schools are large and it is likely that, except for special remedial classes, the less academically able pupils will find themselves in large classes. In such circumstances, there will be few opportunities for pupils to speak and consequently few opportunities to learn how to speak.

4. There is what one university lecturer called the 'authoritarian teaching tradition . . . which stresses silence and the absorption of information rather than the giving out' (т44). This may be a successful form of teaching for certain subjects but it is unlikely

135

to be successful in the communication of speaking skills.[1] The evidence from radio and television suggests that people do not change their speech habits simply by being presented with a model to imitate. In fact, over the years it has been the BBC's standards of pronunciation that have changed rather than those of the listeners.

5. There is a contrast between the speech of the teacher and that of some of the pupils. If an intelligent undergraduate can feel inhibited in university tutorials because she thinks other people have 'cultured accents' (see the remarks by T26, chapter 8), may it not be the case that secondary school pupils also feel inhibited because of the teacher's speech? This is only one aspect of a very complex question, and it is related to the next point.

6. There is resistance on the part of some pupils to the notion of 'talking posh'. However, it is important not to view this resistance in simplistic terms, as mere intransigence. It may be worth quoting again the sensitive remarks of one secondary school teacher:

> They don't feel that proper speech is irrelevant. If you pushed them they would say it was superior. It is valuable, but it is suspect because they are reaching into regions which they haven't entered before and this could be in certain circumstances, getting above yourself. They have a bit of guilt about it, that this is the sort of speech which they should be using in an ideal world. Not a genuine contempt for the mode of speech but a general wariness about it. (T23)

There is also the statement of one of the training college lecturers who had consciously changed his manner of speaking: 'I come from a working-class family and I didn't want to cause difficulty with them, putting on airs and graces, so I had to tread carefully (T41). However, he entered the army on leaving school and made the change away from his family (see chapter 8).

Such factors are, of course, not unique to Glasgow. It is probably true that most large cities in Britain would show a similar set of conditions: emphasis on written work and examinations, large classes, teacher-dominated classrooms, a contrast between the speech habits. However, Glasgow seems to provide a fairly extreme example of the conditions and thus may offer a good situation in which to study what is a widespread problem both in Britain and in the United States.

[1] Ballantyne (1973, 90) states that 77% of the pupils in his survey agreed with the statement 'I get fed up with teachers telling you what you can do and can't do' and 63% agreed with the statement 'Teachers forget you are growing up and always treat you like kids'. While it is true that Ballantyne put the words in the pupils' mouths, as it were, and while it may be equally significant that not all of the pupils agreed with the statements, it is likely that his figures do represent some dissatisfaction with teaching methods.

136

10. Conclusion

She always seemed to pay a lot of attention to me – she
seemed to pay a lot of attention to everyone.
A ten-year-old boy (009) describing a good teacher

AT THE END OF the previous chapter, it was suggested that
the problems with regard to language in the schools, far from being
unique to Glasgow, may be found in many other communities.
This final chapter will look at some of the wider implications of
the Glasgow study. For example, Creber, in his book *Lost for
Words* (1972, 173), which grew out of the discussions at an international seminar on 'The Language of Failure', says that he has
tried '. . . to show the way in which we place not merely a minority
but perhaps a majority of children at a disadvantage through the
kinds of language environment we provide for them.' The evidence
from the Glasgow study certainly offers support for this view.

What can be done to improve the situation? Or, to put it another
way, how can language be made the key that opens the door to
learning for all pupils instead of one that locks it shut for too many
of them? A solution to this problem is crucial for a democratic
educational system, since it is clear that the chances of being shut
out are greater the further down the social scale the pupil stands
(Davie, Butler and Goldstein 1972; Ford 1969; Little and Westergaard 1964). In fact, the roots of the problem may lie in the failure
of the teacher training programmes to adapt to the change from an
élitist and authoritarian system of education to a more democratic
one, and nowhere is this failure more dangerous than in dealing
with language. As the writers of the Bullock Report (1975, 8)
observe: 'If a teacher is to control the growth of competence he
must be able to examine the verbal interaction of a class or group
in terms of an explicit understanding of the operation of language.
We believe that because of their training this is precisely what many
teachers lack. . . .' Moreover, many teachers may not even be
aware of any shortcomings in this respect: 'It is easy for us as
teachers to admit that we need to know more about mathematics.
But because we all talk, we assume that we're all experts on
language' (Cazden 1971, 122).

In the absence of adequate training there is a danger that the
teacher will resort to a traditional approach that will not meet the
most pressing linguistic needs of the pupils. How such a tradition
is perpetuated was beautifully summed up by a ten-year-old boy in

response to a question as to how he would get the children to learn if he were a teacher: 'First of all, I'd start by telling them how to read and write. Tell them not to talk in the class, and all this. Then start them off with arithmetic, two and two, and one and one, and that. Then, if they were good I'd get me a packet of chocolate sweets and give them one' (013). An emphasis on reading, writing and arithmetic, with rewards for being good by not talking in class; it is perhaps too close to the truth to be really amusing. Another ten-year-old, in answer to a query about what her class was doing in English, replied: 'We get apostrophe *s* and inverted commas' (012). Of course, correct punctuation (like correct spelling and polite table manners) is one of the signs of a proper upbringing and deserves attention in the curriculum, but it is a question of priorities. It would be most unfortunate if time devoted to such relatively unimportant matters were allowed to squeeze out attention to more fundamental linguistic skills.

However, as Creber points out (1972, 25), it is not simply a matter of teaching English:

> It is time we abandoned the idea that 'it's up to the English teacher'. It isn't, it hasn't ever been, it never will be. We have thought a good deal about the functions of the school but how much attention have we paid to it as a language environment? In even the latest curriculum schemes what signs are there of language receiving the attention it deserves, what signs of a language policy emerging that would run across the whole curriculum? We remain marvellously unaware of our own language in the classroom: our conscious purposes seem to an objective observer to have little connection with our own speech behaviour and its effect on those we profess to teach. Often we are merely teaching children to play games without meaning, and it is a tribute to their basic kindness that they humour us for so many hours a week, for year after year.

Barnes (1971), in his analysis of lessons given in the first term of secondary education, illustrates very clearly the difficulties many teachers face in trying to avoid playing meaningless games with language in the classroom. He emphasises the need to allow the pupils to speak (pp.61–2):

> . . . the teacher's task should not be to introduce a new set of linguistic forms, but to help his pupils to use language to organize experience in a new way.
>
> Here lies the importance of pupil participation. It is when the pupil is required to use language to grapple with new experience or to order old experience in a new way that he is most likely to find it necessary to use language differently. And this will be very different from taking over someone else's

138

language in external imitation of its forms: on the contrary, it is the very first step towards new patterns of thinking and feeling, new ways of representing reality to himself. . . . It is not enough for pupils to imitate the forms of teachers' language as if they were models to be copied; it is only when they 'try it out' in reciprocal exchanges so that they modify the way they use language to organize reality that they are able to find new functions for language in thinking and feeling. This would suggest that the low level of pupil participation in these lessons, if they are at all typical of secondary lessons, is a matter of some educational urgency. All teachers might well contemplate the classroom implications of this.

In the same volume, Rosen also observes (p.127):

. . . it is as talkers, questioners, arguers, gossips, chatterboxes, that our pupils do much of their most important learning. Their everyday talking voices are the most subtle and versatile means they possess for making sense of what they do and for making sense of others, including their teachers.

It is also necessary for the teacher to listen to what the pupil is saying: '. . . what is clear is that unless the teacher listens to the child and gains some picture of the ways in which he uses language, deliberate efforts may not, in fact, help the child to gain anything' (Tough 1973, 65). Tough is referring to the primary school situation while Barnes and Rosen are considering the secondary school classrooms, but all three comments are relevant to both school situations. The first priority probably is to get away from what Freire (1972) has called a 'digestive' system of education, in which the pupils are 'fed' information that they must 'absorb'. Although there is nowadays much more emphasis on an active role for the pupil (e.g. Riddell and Gulland 1975), there were few signs in the Glasgow study that the teachers were fully aware of the importance of allowing their pupils the opportunity to learn through talking. Since, in Glasgow at least and probably elsewhere, most of the teachers are products of the system in which they teach, it would not be surprising to find that a traditional approach is self-perpetuating. Just as those who extol the values of examinations are often those who have succeeded through passing examinations, similarly, those who have been educated in a system that did not put a high value on talking may feel that talking is not very important. In her survey of primary schools in England Connie Rosen remarks: 'All the teachers I met in schools or in teachers' centres or on courses felt that talk was central to learning, that children need to express themselves in talk and that our aim in school was to help them to become confident users of the spoken language' (Rosen and Rosen 1973, 42).

The evidence of the Glasgow survey suggests that while many teachers might agree with this statement, in practice few of them would give talking as high a priority as this statement implies and those few are more likely to be primary school teachers than secondary school teachers. Yet if school leavers are to be 'confident users of the spoken language' the secondary school also has a part to play. Let us suppose, however, for the purposes of argument, that teachers and administrators are agreed that 'talk is central to learning'.

The main problem is how best to develop adult speech behaviour in adolescents within the school system. There are many pupils who learn this outside of the school, and some teachers feel that the school can do little in comparison with the benefits of a suitable home background. Such a view is convenient for the school because it means that the school has no responsibility for this aspect of the pupil's development. It is possible for teachers who are of this opinion to take a very tolerant attitude towards their pupils' speech. Such a teacher might say:

> I don't attempt to change the way my pupils speak because they have a right to speak the way they wish. If I tried to change their speech I might make them feel that their way of speaking is inferior and I don't want to do that. Instead, I try to present a suitable model by the way I speak to them. Those who wish to change their speech can easily do so by imitating me and their other teachers.

This is probably not too far from the sentiments of many of the teachers who were interviewed and, on the surface, it appears to be a very enlightened attitude.[1] However, if looked at from the point of view of a working-class boy it may appear rather different. The boy will be aware that the teacher speaks differently from him and his friends. The teacher's way of speaking is supported by the authority of the school and the prestige of the educational establishment. However much the boy rejects the values of the school it will be hard for him not to feel that his way of speaking is inferior. As he grows up there will be many occasions on which he is made to feel that others 'speak better' than he does. Although the teacher has not said that the boy's way of speaking is stigmatised, neither has he gone out of his way to give the boy confidence in his way of speaking.

However, even if the working-class boy sees the advantages of the teacher's way of speaking, it is not easy for him to model his speech on the teacher's. Since the teacher's speech is identified with

[1] The writers of the Bullock Report, for example, share this view: 'We believe that a child's accent should be accepted, and that to attempt to suppress it is irrational and neither humane nor necessary' (p.143).

the authority of the school, the boy cannot move closer to that model without, to some extent, abandoning his loyalty to his peer-group. This probably accounts for some of the resistance to 'talking posh'. But there is an even more important sense in which the boy may find it difficult to use the teacher as a model. Most of the teacher's speech in the classroom is administrative speech directed towards maintaining control of the situation. If the boy were to address the teacher in the way the teacher addresses him, he would probably be considered guilty of insolence. This is where the question of authority and discipline are relevant to the development of speaking ability in the pupils.

In most schools, communication between teacher and pupil is not usually of the kind that provides an example of well-mannered and effective conversational exchange between equals. One of the commonest definitions of a good teacher from the ten-year-olds was 'one who doesn't shout at you too much'. However, it is not simply a matter of shouting; there are other weapons, such as ridicule and sarcasm, that are a constant temptation to the person in authority.[1] Such modes of speaking do not provide a model for the pupil in his role *qua* pupil (though, alas, they may influence his behaviour in later life) and they do not help to create an atmosphere in which good-mannered conversation can take place. Moreover, since manners are reciprocal, the only response of the pupil to the authoritarian manner of the teacher may be passive resistance in the form of reticence or minimal speech. The authoritarian structure of the school emphasises the gulf between teacher and pupil and this gulf is greater in the secondary school because of the greater risks if things get out of hand.

There was some resistance on the part of the teachers to suggestions that the system is authoritarian. Some teachers thought that the schools were not particularly authoritarian, while others argued that an authoritarian system is unavoidable in the circumstances.[2] This is a controversial subject for an outsider to comment on but the question is so closely related to the development of adult speech behaviour that it cannot be ignored. One of the depressing experiences for the interviewer was to hear ten-year-olds asserting that it would be impossible to run a school without corporal punishment. This is a particular difficulty with a system that has been in opera-

---

[1] One fifteen-year-old boy described a teacher he disliked: 'He was very overpowering. He liked to take you apart in class. He'd give you a showing up in front of the rest of the boys. I thought that was kind of bad because some of the boys were quite good, nice boys, and he'd make them look like – em – devils, because he didn't like them' (011).

[2] Ballantyne (1973, 96) points out that 26% of the pupils in his survey, in response to an open-ended question about their school, complained that discipline was too strict.

tion for a long time and appears to be working satisfactorily: both teachers and pupils accept it as normal and inevitable. Yet the dependence on corporal punishment is an admission of failure in the school system, since it does not provide a preparation for participation in the adult world of employment. No matter how angry employers may be with their employees they cannot use violence to discipline them. This fact is not irrelevant to the question of speech, since adult speech behaviour is related to adult behaviour in general.

The results of the Glasgow study can be considered cause for alarm but not despair. Even the least articulate children interviewed were able to talk coherently and interestingly once the right question had been asked. Similarly, even the least forthcoming teachers interviewed showed concern for the welfare of their pupils. Thus the roots of the problem appear to lie not in the inability of the pupils to learn or in the indifference of the teachers but in the complexity of the situation in which both teachers and pupils find themselves. The problem will not be solved in any particular situation by calling in 'experts' from the outside who are expected to bring with them already packaged answers to every question. Nor can the teachers themselves be expected to deal with the problem on their own, partly because of lack of time and resources, and partly because they may be too close to their own particular situation to see the larger picture. As Riddell and Gullard (1975) point out, in connection with currciulum development, the solution may lie in bringing together the knowledge gained by teachers from their personal experience with the more theoretical knowledge and perspective provided by specialists in a particular field.

To a certain extent the present work represents such a collaboration. As is obvious from the comments cited in chapter 8 the observations of teachers at all levels have contributed greatly to the conclusions reached in the Glasgow study. At the same time, in the course of the interviews with the teachers the interviewer often felt as if he were acting as a catalyst, producing reactions that the teachers themselves were not fully conscious of until the appropriate question evoked them. The suggestions for tackling the problem that are given below are thus not the investigator's alone but those that emerged from the discussions with the teachers, and it would be hard to disentangle the strands to apportion either credit or blame. Although they come as recommendations made with specific reference to the Glasgow situation, it is likely that they will be relevant, *mutatis mutandis*, to a wide variety of different situations.

1. Ample opportunities for drama and debating should be pro-

vided. In many schools this is already being done, and it would be relatively simple to increase these opportunities by allowing a few more class hours and employing additional qualified personnel. However, these activities will have at best a small impact on the total situation, so it may be worth while explaining why they should be the first recommendation. There are three reasons. The first is that there are recognised techniques for developing competence in the skills required for such activities. It is thus possible to select staff on the basis of their qualifications to teach these skills. Secondly, the introduction of these activities, where they are not already a regular part of the curriculum, need not disturb or involve other members of staff, though, of course, they may choose to become involved. Thirdly, drama and debating are worthwhile activities in their own right and not simply as a means to the end of confidence in the use of spoken language. For all these reasons, greater emphasis on drama and debating should be encouraged.

2. The question of social judgements about language, particularly about accent, should be openly discussed in school, instead of being treated as a taboo subject even less mentionable than sex or money. The best place to do this would probably be in the English classroom, where it could form part of the study of the English language. There is no reason why the attention of pupils should not be drawn to the differences in the way people speak and to the complex historical and social conditions that produced these differences. In the past, discussion of dialect differences at an elementary level might have been hampered by the rather cumbersome and repellent system of phonetic transcription necessary to illustrate the differences, but nowadays with tapes and records and the wide variety of accents broadcast on radio and television there is ample material to illustrate different forms of speech. The difficulty is more likely to lie in the inhibitions of the English teacher, for it is probable that few teachers will have been adequately trained in the history of the language or in the description of contemporary English. This is something that could be remedied by the provision of suitable textbooks and some in-service training. A more serious problem is the teacher's own speech development. Many teachers will have changed their own way of speaking at some time, and for some it may even have been a rather traumatic experience at training college, to judge from certain comments in the interviews. Teachers might find it hard to discuss their own speech with pupils, particularly since this is not a normal topic of discussion in the classroom. Yet honesty in this matter might be the key to the pupils' understanding of the complex values that apply in social judgements about speech. It is clearly a situation that would demand tact, understanding and frankness from the teacher,

and the discussion would inevitably impinge upon topics such as snobbery and social inequality, which are not the easiest to handle in the classroom. However, avoiding the question of social judgements about speech simply means that it is a matter of chance whether the school-leaver knows the standards by which he may be assessed in looking for employment. It should be emphasised that what is being advocated here is not speech training or elocution lessons. Such approaches are likely to be ineffectual at best, if not actually harmful. Nor is it being suggested that the aim of discussing speech differences should be to encourage the pupils to speak in a certain manner. On the contrary, one of the principal aims should be to make clear to pupils that their speech is not a degenerate form of language but has a long and respectable history. However, it is also a mistake to be sentimental about traditional varieties of speech which are held in low esteem by influential members of the community. More precise information about the kinds of features that distinguish dialects might be helpful to any pupils who may wish at some later date to modify their speech in the direction of a more prestigious variety. The important thing is that the pupils should be in possession of the information that will allow them to make a conscious choice about the way they speak. At the moment, the schools appear to assume that the pupils have this knowledge. The evidence of the present survey, indirect though much of it is, suggests that the pupils would benefit from more open discussion of speech differences.

3. The problem of instilling confidence in the use of spoken language should not be seen as the responsibility of the English department or the Drama department alone: it is a problem that concerns all the teachers in the school. Ideally, in every classroom every effort should be made to encourage natural, informal, polite conversational exchange between teacher and pupil, and between pupil and pupil. In practice, it is hard to imagine this happening on a wide scale in Glasgow. Partly this is because of class size but more probably it is because teacher and pupil are socialised at an early stage into their traditional roles. To break into the cycle would be to risk confusion and disorder for the sake of what may seem an intangible reward. Yet until a change takes place it is likely that the 'traditional' lack of confidence in speaking will continue. If talk really is central to learning then the major aim of educational planners, school administrator, training college lecturers and the teachers themselves should be to find ways in which talking can take place in the classroom. Class size provides an illustration. If it is the case that, in the present atmosphere in schools, rational discourse can only take place in small groups, then the curriculum must be arranged to make sure that all pupils regularly have some

classes with small numbers.[1] The classes should be in all subjects, not simply special discussion groups set up with no other purpose in mind. This is an organisational problem but it is not insurmountable and some schools are already experimenting with such programmes. However, the necessary reorganisation will only take place if the importance of speech is recognised and the need to instil confidence in speaking is given the highest priority.

4. The teacher training colleges could do more to stress the importance of speech. Since the spoken language is fundamental to teaching (otherwise it could be carried out by correspondence course or by a machine) it might have been expected that one of the central concerns of the training colleges would have been the study of oral communication. This does not appear to be the case, judging from the comments of teachers. There are probably historical reasons for this. In the past, in one of the teacher training colleges at least, speech training meant speech correction and there has been an understandable reaction against this. Moreover, the fluctuating fashions in theoretical linguistics have not made it easy for the applied linguist to know what he can apply where. As a result there is very little that can be passed on to the prospective teacher as doctrine, and that little is likely to be out of date or misleading. However, this should not be the aim of the training colleges, in any case. Instead, they should treat the question of communication as problematic and discuss with the students, who are largely the products of the local educational system, what it is that interferes with communication in the classroom.

5. There should be in-service training in language provided, not only for teachers of English but for all teachers at both primary and secondary levels. The question that then arises is: What does in-service training in language consist of? As was mentioned in the previous section there is not much point in training teachers in theoretical linguistics. Some background information on Scottish English might be useful and this would not be too difficult to pro-

[1] Cf. Creber (1972, 83): 'What continued acceptance of oversize classes means for language in the classroom needs to be spelt out. Large numbers force upon the teacher an authoritarian role so that for most of the time the child becomes a receiver of only generalized, i.e. impersonal, language; the possibility of warm 'individuated' chat is reduced. This restriction on the way in which the teacher can relate to individuals within the class has two further consequences: in the first place, his potential as a listener and as a partner or participator, working alongside a child or small group of children, is drastically reduced; secondly, he is prevented from discovering enough about individuals to prescribe appropriately (reading material for example), and diversification of activity becomes progressively more difficult. All this means a drastic limitation of the range of linguistic experience the child can hope for in the classroom and this must have various effects upon his learning.'

145

vide. There are a number of recent works on sociolinguistics that could provide a starting point for discussions. The major emphasis should be on attitudes towards language among the teachers and in the community. This is a necessary preliminary to any discussion with pupils in the classroom. However, probably the most useful contribution to in-service training could be made by a social psychologist interested in small group communication. It is the dynamics of personal interaction within the group that are crucial to the success of a discussion group. In-service training along these lines would probably do more good than any purely linguistic training. Essentially, the problem of inarticulateness or lack of confidence in speaking is not a linguistic problem but a psychological one, for the teachers as well as the pupils. In order to encourage adult behaviour, including adult speech behaviour, it is necessary to allow the pupils the freedom to make mistakes, otherwise they are merely role-playing. However, to allow too much freedom in some schools would be to risk chaos. The fear of things getting out of hand clearly inhibits many teachers who would temperamentally be willing to permit a more relaxed atmosphere in the classroom. The aim of the in-service training should be to give the teachers the confidence that will encourage them to take a few more risks in allowing their pupils 'to talk back'.

The above suggestions have been put forward on the assumption that everyone agrees that talk is central to learning. Clearly there is at present no such agreement in Glasgow. Some teachers and employers were worried about what might have to be given up if more attention were paid to speech, and there is the general view that examinations, for all their obvious shortcomings, are the only worthwhile test of academic achievement. This is not the place in which to argue for the importance of speech but two points may be made briefly in response. In the first place, it does not follow that an emphasis on the spoken language must be at the expense of something else. Talking should not be thought of as a separate subject, which appears in the curriculum as such. On the contrary, it is a means of learning any subject whether it is science, history or accountancy. Secondly, it is clear that the emphasis on examinations benefits most those who are successful in the examinations. This is the function of examinations and there is no point in deploring it. However, for those who are unsuccessful, and they are a majority of the early school-leavers, the emphasis upon examinations has meant concentrating on failure. This can hardly give them confidence to go out into the world of employment. An educational system that made them more confident users of the spoken language would give them something that employers are looking for. It might even help them to pass examinations.

146

Appendix A. List of Informants

Community Sample: Ten-year-olds

No.	Sex	Religion	Class	Employment[1]
009	M	Catholic	I	Teacher of accounting in a Further Education College
021	M	Protestant	I	Chief draughtsman
022	F	Protestant	I	Managing director of a whisky bond
046	F	Protestant	I	Civil engineer
013	M	Protestant	IIa	Draughtsman
014	M	Protestant	IIa	Engineering inspector
008	F	Catholic	IIa	Salesman
012	F	Protestant	IIa	Collection salesman
035	M	Catholic	IIb	Security guard
018	M	Protestant	IIb	Electrical engineer
053	F	Protestant	IIb	Machine shop engineer
016	F	Protestant	IIb	Electrician
005	M	Protestant	III	Unemployed manual worker
007	M	Protestant	III	Lorry driver
033	F	Catholic	III	Labourer
006	F	Protestant	III	Slater, roadmender

Additional Informants

No.	Sex	Religion	Class	Employment[1]
017	F	Protestant	I/IIa	Skipper for Clyde Port Authority
034	M	Catholic	III	Cleansing Department worker

Community Sample: Fifteen-year-olds

No.	Sex	Religion	Class	Employment[1]
004	M	Protestant	I	Consultant dental surgeon
049	M	Protestant	I	Director of family business
031	F	Protestant	I	Doctor
037	F	Catholic	I	Depute head teacher
011	M	Catholic	IIa	Tax officer, higher grade
029	M	Protestant	IIa	Police constable
020	F	Fundamentalist	IIa	Commercial artist
051	F	Protestant	IIa	Sub-editor
026	M	Protestant	IIb	Machine shop engineer
024	M	Protestant	IIb	Blacksmith, maintenance worker
025	F	Protestant	IIb	Radial-arm driller

[1] For 10- and 15-year-olds, the parent's employment.

No.	Sex	Religion	Class	Employment
052	F	Protestant	IIb	Joiner
001	M	Catholic	III	Labourer
041	M	Protestant	III	Fruit market porter
002	F	Catholic	III	Boilerman in public baths
042	F	Protestant	III	Lorry driver

Additional Informants

003	F	Protestant	I/IIa	Manager of Works in docks
038	F	Protestant	IIb/III	Traffic warden
043	M	Catholic	IIb	Electrician

Community Sample: Adults

015	M	Catholic	I	Depute head teacher
050	M	Protestant	I	Director of family business
030	F	Protestant	I	Doctor
045	F	Protestant	I	Civil engineer
010	M	Catholic	IIa	Tax officer, higher grade
028	M	Protestant	IIa	Police constable
019	F	Fundamentalist	IIa	Commercial artist
036	F	Protestant	IIa	Collector salesman
040	M	Protestant	IIb	Radial-arm driller
032	M	Protestant	IIb	Electrician
023	F	Protestant	IIb	Blacksmith, maintenance worker
047	F	Catholic	IIb	Electrician
048	M	Protestant	III	Lorry driver
027	M	Catholic	III	Cleansing Department worker, recently promoted to supervisor
044	F	Protestant	III	Fruit market porter
054	F	Protestant	III	Factory worker

Additional Informant

039	F	Protestant	IIb/III	Traffic warden

Teachers Sample

No.	Sex	Employment
T01	M	Senior Lecturer, Biochemistry, University
T02	M	Senior Lecturer, Primary Education, Training College
T03	M	Lecturer, Chemical Engineering, University
T04	M	Senior Lecturer, Mechanics of Laterals, University
T05	M	Lecturer, Education, Training College
T06	F	Lecturer, Drama, University
T07	M	English Teacher, Secondary School
T08	M	Assistant Head, & Guidance, Secondary School
T09	F	French & German Teacher, Secondary School
T10	F	English Teacher, Secondary School
T11	F	Primary II Teacher, Primary School
T12	F	Primary III Teacher, Primary School
T13	F	Senior Pupils' Teacher, Primary School
T14	F	Senior Pupils' Teacher, Primary School
T15	M	Principal PE Teacher, Secondary School
T16	M	Science Teacher, Secondary School
T17	F	Guidance & English Teacher, Secondary School
T18	F	Geography Teacher, Secondary School
T19	F	Primary Teacher, Primary School
T20	F	Primary Teacher, Primary School
T21	F	Primary Teacher, Primary School
T22	F	Primary Teacher, Primary School
T23	M	Senior English Teacher, Secondary School
T24	M	Classics Teacher, Secondary School
T25	F	English & Guidance Teacher, Secondary School
T26	F	French & German Teacher, Secondary School
T27	F	Lecturer, Social Work, Training College
T28	M	Senior Teacher, Primary School
T29	M	Teacher, Primary School
T30	F	Infant I Teacher, Primary School
T31	F	Teacher, Primary School
T32	F	Teacher, Primary School
T33	F	Teacher, Primary School
T34	F	Teacher, Primary School
T35	M	Teacher, Primary School
T36	F	Classics Teacher, Secondary School
T37	M	Drama Teacher, Secondary School
T38	F	Remedial Teacher, Secondary School
T39	M	Senior English Teacher, Secondary School
T40	M	Lecturer, English, University
T41	F	Lecturer, Educational Technology, Training College
T42	M	Lecturer, English, Training College

No.	Sex	Employment
T43	M	Vice-Principal, Training College
T44	F	Lecturer, Science, Training College
T45	M	Lecturer, Education, University
T46	F	Lecturer, English, Training College
T47	F	Senior Lecturer, Mathematics, University
T48	M	Lecturer, Law, University

Employers Sample

E01	Staff Manageress, national chain of department stores
E02	Staff Manager, national engineering firm
E03a	Personnel Manager, national engineering firm
E03b	Assistant Staff Manager, national engineering firm
E04	Personnel Manager, national manufacturing firm
E05	Assistant Staff Manager, Scottish bank
E06	Personnel Manager, firm of chartered accountants
E07	Staff Manageress, local factory
E08a	Staff Manager, engineering firm
E08b	Assistant Staff Manager, engineering firm
E09	Personnel Manager, national insurance company
E10	University Administrator responsible for technical staff
E11a	University Administrator responsible for secretarial staff
E11b	University Administrator responsible for secretarial staff
E12	Senior Administrator, Centre for Secretarial Studies
E13	Administrative Assistant to Medical Faculty
E14	Staff Manager, marketing firm
E15a	Establishments Officer, Glasgow Corporation
E15b	Establishments Officer, Glasgow Corporation
E16	Personnel Manager, local factory
E17a	Inland Revenue Officer concerned with recruitment
E17b	Inland Revenue Officer concerned with recruitment
E18	Senior Medical Faculty Administrator
E19	Staff Manager, local factory
E20	Managing Director, car distributors
E21	Careers Officer, Glasgow Corporation
E22a	Managing Director, local employment agency
E22b	Assistant Manageress, local employment agency

Appendix B. Questionnaires

Ten-year-olds

1 Family Background
  1.1 When were you born?
    1.11 Where?
    1.12 Have you always lived here?
  1.2 How many are there in your family?
    1.21 What does your father do?
2 Personal Memories
  2.1 What's your earliest memory?
  2.2 Who's your best friend?
    2.21 What do you like about him/her?
  2.3 What do you do when you're not in school?
  2.4 What's the best present you've ever had?
  2.5 Do you have a dog/any animals?
  2.6 Have you ever been really scared?
    2.61 Have you ever been badly hurt/to hospital?
  2.7 Can you tell me something funny that happened to you (or sad)?
  2.8 Have you travelled outside of Glasgow?
    2.81 Which way do you like to travel best?
3 Games
  3.1 What games do you play?
    M 3.11 Did you ever play marbles? What games did you play?
    F 3.12 Can you repeat for me any rhymes you say when skipping? (Suggest an example or two if necessary.)
  3.2 What do you say when you want to stop the game? (Keys?)
  3.3 How do you decide who's 'het' at the start of a game? (Counting rhymes? 'One potato, two potato . . .'? Do you know any more?)
4 Schooling
  4.1 Can you remember your first day at school? If not, what's your earliest memory of school?
  4.2 What are you doing in school today?
    4.21 Do you like reading?
    4.22 What are you reading?
  4.3 Have you ever had a teacher you hated? If so, why?
    4.31 What makes a good teacher?

4.4 What kind of school would you like if you were setting up a new one?

    4.41 If you were a teacher, how would you get the pupils to learn?

4.5 Do you think you could run a school without using the belt?

5 Aspirations

5.1 What do you want to do when you leave school?

    5.11 What would you have to do in order to do that?

5.2 What would you do if you were rich?

6 Nationality

6.1 If someone asked you what nationality you are, what would you say? (British, Scottish.)

    6.11 Would you mind if you heard someone referring to you as English?

6.2 Do you think there's much difference between the Scots and the English?

7 Glasgow

7.1 If you knew someone was coming to live in Glasgow, would you tell him this is a good place to live?

    7.11 Is there much fighting round here?

8 Entertainment

8.1 Do you like watching TV?

    8.11 What were you watching yesterday?

9 Language

9.1 Do you think it's a good thing that people speak differently in different parts of the country?

10 One of the things we're interested in is the different ways that people speak. I wonder if you would mind reading out a few sentences for me.

Now here are some words that sometimes sound the same. Could you read them out for me.

Fifteen-year-olds

1 Family background

1.1 When were you born?

    1.11 Where?

    1.12 Have you lived anywhere else? Where?

1.2 Where are your parents from?

    1.21 Do you know where your grandparents came from?

1.3 What does your father do?

    1.31 Does anyone else in your family work?

1.4 Have you any brothers or sisters?

    1.41 What other relatives do you see regularly?

2 Personal Memories
  2.1 What's the first thing you can remember doing?
    2.11 What was the best present you ever got?
  2.2 Who's the best friend you ever had? Tell me about him/her.
    2.21 What kind of person do you like to be friends with?
  2.3 What do you like to do best when you're not in school?
    (Ask for an example.)
  2.4 Have you ever had to eat something you can't stand?
    What happened?
  2.5 Did you ever get into hot water when it wasn't your
    fault. What happened?
  2.6 Is there much fighting around here?
    2.61 Do you think there's less fighting in Glasgow than
      there used to be?
3 Games
  3.1 What games do you play? (Ask for details.)
    M 3.12 Did you ever play marbles? What games did you
      play?
    F 3.12 Can you repeat for me any rhymes you (used to)
      say when skipping? (Suggest an example or two,
      if necessary.)
  3.2 What do/did you say when you want(ed) to stop a game?
    (Keys?)
  3.3 How do/did you decide who's 'het' at the start of a game?
    Counting rhymes? 'One potato, two potato . . .'? Do you
    know any more?
4 Schooling
  4.1 Do you remember your first day at school? If not, what's
    your earliest memory of school?
  4.2 Were you happy at primary school?
    4.21 What do you feel about this school?
    4.22 When do you want to leave school?
    4.23 What do you like doing at school?
  4.3 If you were starting a school from scratch what would
    you want it to be like?
  4.4 If you were a teacher, how would you get the pupils to
    learn?
  4.5 Did you ever have a teacher you really hated? Tell me
    about him/her. (If not, one you really liked.)
    4.51 What makes a good teacher?
  4.6 Do you think there is anything parents can do to help
    their children do well in school? (If yes, what?)
  4.7 What do you think of going to school till sixteen?
  4.8 Do you think you could run a school without using the
    belt?

4.9 Should pupils have more say in the running of the school?

5   Aspirations
   5.1 What do you want to do when you leave school? (If appropriate) What do you need to know in order to do that?
   5.2 What does it take to get ahead in life?
   5.3 Suppose you had a choice of three jobs: a high paying job that might not last for long, a medium paying job with a 50–50 chance of losing it, a low paying job, but with plenty of security. Which would you go for? Why?
   5.4 Do you think it makes a difference how you speak for getting a job? For all jobs?
      5.41 What makes you speak the way you do? (Home, school, friends?)
   5.5 If you could get a better job by changing the way you speak, would you do it? (If no, why not?)
   5.6 What would you do if someone gave you £1000?

6   Nationality
   6.1 If someone asked you what nationality you are, what would you say? British? Scottish?
      6.11 Would you be annoyed if you heard a foreigner referring to you as English?
   6.2 Do you think there's much difference between the Scots and the English?
   6.3 Would you go to England to get a better job?
      6.31 To another country?
   6.4 Should Scotland have its own Parliament?

7   Glasgow
   7.1 They say Glasgow used to be a very tough place with all the fighting that went on. Is it still like that?
   7.2 If you knew someone who was thinking of coming to live in Glasgow would you tell him it was a good place to live? Why?
   7.3 They say you can always recognise someone from Glasgow by the way he speaks. Do you think that's true?
      7.31 Could you tell which part of Glasgow he comes from?
   7.4 Do you think it's a good thing that people speak differently in different parts of the country? Why?
   7.5 Would you say that Glasgow people are snobbish?

8   Religion
   8.1 Do you go to church regularly? Where?
   8.2 Do you think the church is doing enough to attract young people?

8.3 Do you think it's possible for a Catholic and a Protestant to be friends? To get married?

9 Entertainment
    9.1 Are you interested in football? Do you think any team can stop Celtic?
    9.2 What do you think can be done about the violence at football matches?
    9.3 Do you think all the violence on TV leads to juvenile delinquency?
        9.31 Do you think TV ever has a good influence?
    9.4 What TV shows do you watch?
        9.41 Would you rather watch something on TV than be there where it's happening?

10 They say that a lot of the old words are never used nowadays. I'd like to ask you if you've ever heard some of them.

11 One of the things we're interested in is in the different ways that people speak. I wonder if you'd mind reading out a few sentences for me.
Now here are some words that sometimes sound the same. Could you read them out for me.

Adults

1 Family Background
    1.1 When were you born?
        1.11 Where?
        1.12 Have you lived anywhere else? Where?
    1.2 Where did your parents come from?
    1.3 What did your father do?
        1.31 Did anyone else in your family work when you were growing up?
   *1.4 Where is your husband/wife from?
        1.41 How many children have you?

2 Personal Memories
    2.1 What is your earliest memory?
    2.2 Where did you go to school?
        2.21 How far did you go?
     *2.22 Did your family ever say they wanted you to stay on at school?
    2.3 Looking back on it, what do you think of the kind of schooling you got? What changes would you have wanted?
        2.31 Did you ever feel that you were unfairly punished as a child? What happened?

  * where appropriate

*2.4 Were you friends with anyone who did well at school?
If yes, tell me about him/her. Do you know what
happened to him/her when he/she left school?

*2.5 What was the worst trouble you got into as a child?

2.6 Do you think things have changed much since you were
at school? For the better or for the worse?

    2.61 Do you think there is anything parents can do to
help their children do well in school? (If yes, what?)

    2.62 Do you think a school can be run without corporal
punishment?

2.7 Do you think it's a good idea for all children to stay on
at school until they're sixteen?

2.8 Was there much fighting in your part of town? Have
things got better or worse?

2.9 What kind of things did you do when you weren't in
school and there wasn't TV to watch?

    2.91 Can you remember any games you used to play?

    2.92 What did you say when you wanted to stop a game?
(Keys?)

    2.93 How did you decide who was 'het' at the start of a
game? Counting rhymes? 'One potato, two
potato . . .'? Do you remember any more?

    2.94 What did you say for staying away from school
without permission? (Plunking?)

3   Occupation

3.1 What was your first job when you left school? What have
you been doing since then?

3.2 If when you were young you'd a choice of three jobs: a
high paying job with no security, a medium paying job
with a 50–50 chance of losing it, a low paying job that
seemed pretty safe. Which would you have chosen? Why?

3.3 What does it take to get ahead in life?

3.4 What would you advise a young man to do in order to
improve his chances of a good job?

    3.41 A young woman?

3.5 Do you think it makes a difference how you speak for
getting a job? For all jobs?

    3.51 What determines the way you speak – home, school,
friends?

3.6 Do you think Scots people are good workers? (If no, why
not?)

4   Glasgow

4.1 Would you say to someone thinking of moving here that
you can enjoy yourself all right in Glasgow?

4.2 Are Glasgow people friendly? Have they got a good sense of humour?

    4.21 Do people around here go to help someone when he's in trouble?

4.3 What's the biggest change you've seen in Glasgow? On the whole have things got better or worse here?

    4.31 Do you think people in Glasgow are better off now than in the past?

4.4 If you were on the Corporation what would you try to do?

4.5 Do you think Glasgow people are snobbish? (If yes, what about people around here?)

4.6 People often talk about there being different (social) classes – do you think this is true in Glasgow?

    4.61 How many classes are there?

    4.62 Where do you put yourself?

    4.63 What is it that determines which class you belong to – family, money, job?

5   Religion

5.1 Do you go to church regularly? Where?

5.2 Do you think the church is doing a good job of changing to meet modern attitudes?

5.3 Sometimes people say 'Whatever's going to happen is going to happen'. Do you agree with that?

5.4 Have you ever been in a situation where you prayed because you were in danger of getting killed? What happened?

6   Entertainment

*6.1 Do you take an interest in football? Do you think any team will stop Celtic?

    6.11 What do you think can be done about the violence at football matches?

6.2 Do you think that all the violence on TV leads to juvenile delinquency?

    6.21 Do you think that TV has made a difference to the things children know? In what way?

6.3 What TV shows do you like to watch?

7   Nationalism

7.1 If someone asked you what nationality you are, what would you say? British? Scottish?

    7.11 Would you be annoyed if you heard a foreigner referring to you as English?

7.2 Would you say there's much difference between the Scots and the English? Do you think being in the Common Market will make us more like each other?

7.3 Do you think Scotland should have its own Parliament?

7.4 Would you move to England to get a better job?

7.5 Would you mind if your son or daughter married some-one from England and went to live there?

7.6 Have you ever thought of emigrating?

8 Language

8.1 Do you think it's a good thing that people speak differ-ently in different parts of the country?

8.2 They say you can always recognise a Glaswegian by the way he speaks. Do you think that's true?

8.21 Could you tell what part of Glasgow someone comes from?

8.3 Is there anything you don't like about the way people speak around here?

8.31 Do you like the way the Edinburgh people speak better?

8.4 Do you think it's more important for a man or for a woman to speak well?

9 They say that a lot of the old words are never used nowadays. I'd like to ask you if you've ever heard some of them.

10 One of the things we're interested in is the different ways that people speak. I wonder if you'd mind reading out a few sentences for me.

Now here are some words that sometimes sound the same. Could you read them out for me.

Teachers

1 Personal Background

1.1 What did you do after leaving school?

1.11 Where did you do your teacher training?

1.2 What was your first teaching post?

1.21 Where have you taught since then?

1.22 What is your present teaching post?

2 Present School

2.1 What kind of school would you say this is?

*2.11 How does it compare with other schools you've taught in?

2.2 How would you describe the kind of pupils you get at this school? Middle-class? Working-class?

2.3 What do most of the pupils do when they leave?

3 Language

3.1 Have you ever taught pupils who have had language problems?

3.2 Are any of your pupils at a disadvantage because of the way they speak?

    3.21 Is it because of their accent or is it a difficulty in expressing themselves?

3.3 Do you think the school should attempt to change the way pupils speak? If yes, in what ways?

    3.31 Which do you think has the most influence on the way someone speaks: family, school, friends?

3.4 Do you think enough is done to encourage pupils to speak in the school?

3.5 It is often said that English children are more articulate than Scottish children. Do you think that's true? If so, why do you think that should be the case?

3.6 Cliff Hanley said that when he was growing up he and his friends were trilingual; they spoke Standard English in school, good Scots at home, and gutter Glaswegian in the street. Would you say that is still the case?

    3.61 Do you find that your pupils know many of the traditional Scots words?

3.7 Do you think it's a good thing that people speak differently in different parts of the country?

    3.71 Are there any regional accents you dislike?

    3.72 What about Glasgow? Is there anything you don't like about the way people speak in Glasgow?

3.8 Are you conscious that your own speech has changed at any time?

3.9 Do you think any of your pupils are likely to have difficulty in getting the kind of job they want because of the way in which they speak?

Lecturers

1   Personal background

   1.1 Where were you born?

      1.11 When?

      1.12 Have you lived anywhere else? Where?

   1.2 What did your father do?

   1.3 Where did you go to school?

      1.31 Looking back on it, what do you think of the kind of schooling you got?

      1.32 Do you think schools have changed much since you were at school? For the better or the worse?

   1.4 Did you go straight to university when you left school?

   1.5 What was your first teaching post?

     *1.51 Where have you taught since then?

*1.52 What is your present teaching post?
1.6 What made you decide to go into academic life?
  1.61 Did you ever consider any other profession?
2 Present university or college
  2.1 What is the background of most of the students you teach?
    2.11 Would you say they are mainly middle-class/ working-class?
    2.12 What is it that determines which class you belong to: family background, education, income, job?
  2.2 What do most of your students do when they graduate?
    *2.21 What kind of problems do they come up against in finding a job these days?
3 Speech
  3.1 Do you think the way they speak affects their chances of getting a job? In what ways?
  3.2 Do you think that prospective teachers should receive special training in speaking?
  3.3 Is there anything you don't like about the way any of your students speak?
  3.4 If you wanted to suggest a model of pronunciation for your students where would you look: the BBC, the university?
  3.5 They say you can always recognise someone from Glasgow by the way he speaks. Do you think that's true?
    3.51 Could you tell which part of Glasgow he comes from?
    3.52 What is it about Glasgow speech that makes it different from other accents?
    3.53 Are there any regional accents you don't like?
  3.6 Do you think it's a good thing that people speak differently in different parts of the country? Why?
  3.7 When you were growing up or completing your education did you ever feel the need or the desire to modify your own way of speaking?

Employers

1 What kind of people are you looking for?
  1.1 Do you employ many graduates?
2 What kind of qualifications (e.g., 'O' levels, Highers) do you look for?
3 When you are interviewing someone for a job do you pay attention to the way that he speaks?
  3.1 What kind of things do you pay attention to?

160

4   To what extent are you interested in accent?
    4.1 Are there any accents that you would consider unaccept-
        able in an applicant?
5   To what extent are you interested in fluency and the ability
    to express oneself clearly?
6   Do you notice any differences between applicants from
    Glasgow and those from other parts of the country?
7   Do you notice any differences between those who have
    attended fee-paying schools and those who have been to
    state schools?
8   Do you think the educational system is doing a good job in
    providing the kind of people you want?
    8.1 If not, what changes would you like to see?

Appendix C
Percentage of Variants Used by Each Informant

Table 1. Variants of (i) used by adults. In this and subsequent tables the first two speakers in each class are male and the second two female

Class I	Total	(i–1)		(i–2)		(i–3)		(i–4)		(i–5)	
Speaker	tokens	no.	%	no.	%	no.	%	no.	%	no.	%
015	80	24	30.0	40	50.0	13	16.3	3	3.8	0	0.0
050	80	22	27.5	48	60.0	10	12.5	0	0.0	0	0.0
030	80	28	35.0	45	56.3	7	8.8	0	0.0	0	0.0
045	79	47	59.5	30	37.9	2	2.5	0	0.0	0	0.0
mean			38.0		51.1		10.0		0.9		0.0
S.D.			12.7		8.4		5.1		1.6		0.0
Class IIa											
010	42	0	0.0	16	38.1	24	57.1	2	4.8	0	0.0
028	80	0	0.0	32	40.0	37	46.3	11	13.8	0	0.0
019	48	10	20.8	36	75.0	2	4.2	0	0.0	0	0.0
036	50	1	2.0	38	76.0	9	18.0	2	4.0	0	0.0
mean			5.7		57.3		31.4		5.6		0.0
S.D.			8.8		18.2		21.2		5.0		0.0
Class IIb											
032	74	0	0.0	12	16.2	36	48.7	19	25.7	7	9.5
040	80	1	1.3	28	35.0	37	46.3	13	16.3	1	1.3
023	62	0	0.0	22	35.5	32	51.6	8	12.9	0	0.0
047	80	2	2.5	33	41.3	38	47.5	7	8.8	0	0.0
mean			0.9		32.0		48.5		15.9		2.7
S.D.			1.0		9.4		2.0		6.2		3.9
Class III											
027	80	0	0.0	15	18.8	38	47.5	22	27.5	5	6.3
048	80	0	0.0	34	42.5	30	37.5	13	16.3	3	3.8
044	44	1	2.3	19	43.2	21	47.7	2	4.6	1	2..
055	40	1	2.5	18	45.0	15	37.5	5	12.5	1	2.5
mean			1.2		37.4		42.6		15.2		3.7
S.D.			1.2		10.8		5.1		8.3		1.0

Table 2. Variants of (i) used by 15-year-olds

Class I	Total tokens	(i–1)		(i–2)		(i–3)		(i–4)		(i–5)	
Speaker		no.	%	no.	%	no.	%	no.	%	no.	%
004	64	4	6.5	36	58.1	15	24.2	7	11.3	0	0.0
049	70	6	8.6	37	52.9	21	30.0	6	8.6	0	0.0
031	62	14	22.6	47	75.8	1	1.6	0	0.0	0	0.0
037	64	35	54.7	27	42.2	1	1.6	0	0.0	1	1.6
mean			23.1		57.2		14.3		5.0		0.4
s.d.			19.3		12.2		12.9		5.1		0.7
Class IIa											
011	60	1	1.7	30	50.0	24	40.0	5	8.3	0	0.0
029	70	0	0.0	20	28.6	28	40.0	22	31.4	0	0.0
020	40	4	10.0	31	77.5	4	10.0	1	2.5	0	0.0
051	52	6	11.5	33	63.5	8	15.4	5	9.6	0	0.0
mean			5.8		54.9		26.4		13.0		0.0
s.d.			5.0		18.0		13.8		11.0		0.0
Class IIb											
024	42	0	0.0	3	7.1	25	59.5	10	23.8	4	9.5
026	80	2	2.5	26	32.5	36	45.0	15	18.8	1	1.3
025	80	0	0.0	26	32.5	38	47.5	16	20.0	0	0.0
052	38	1	2.6	16	42.1	15	39.5	6	15.8	0	0.0
mean			1.3		28.6		47.9		19.6		2.7
s.d.			1.3		13.0		7.3		2.9		4.0
Class III											
001	40	0	0.0	19	47.5	17	42.5	3	7.5	1	2.5
041	66	0	0.0	20	30.3	25	37.9	12	18.2	9	13.6
002	40	0	0.0	4	10.0	20	50.0	16	40.0	0	0.0
042	39	1	2.6	8	20.5	20	51.3	7	18.0	3	7.7
mean			0.6		27.1		45.4		20.9		6.0
s.d.			1.1		13.8		5.5		11.8		5.2

163

Table 3. Variants of (i) used by 10-year-olds

Class I	Total tokens	(i–1) no.	%	(i–2) no.	%	(i–3) no.	%	(i–4) no.	%	(i–5) no.	%
Speaker											
009	40	1	2.5	32	80.0	6	15.0	1	2.5	0	0.0
021	76	3	4.0	19	25.0	42	55.3	12	15.8	0	0.0
022	80	8	10.0	49	61.3	23	28.8	0	0.0	0	0.0
046	76	13	17.1	44	57.9	17	22.4	2	2.6	0	0.0
mean			8.4		56.0		30.4		5.2		0.0
s.d.			5.8		19.8		15.2		6.2		0.0
Class IIa											
013	72	3	4.2	23	31.9	33	45.8	10	13.9	3	4.2
014	42	0	0.0	15	35.7	16	38.1	7	16.7	4	9.5
008	42	2	4.8	29	69.1	11	26.2	0	0.0	0	0.0
012	78	6	7.7	39	50.0	27	34.6	6	7.7	0	0.0
mean			4.2		46.7		36.2		9.6		3.4
s.d.			2.8		14.6		7.1		6.4		3.9
Class IIb											
018	80	3	3.8	35	43.8	24	30.0	18	22.5	0	0.0
035	72	9	12.5	42	58.3	15	20.8	6	8.3	0	0.0
016	58	0	0.0	14	24.1	33	56.9	11	19.0	0	0.0
053	80	1	1.3	26	32.5	37	46.3	13	16.3	3	3.8
mean			4.4		39.7		38.5		16.5		0.9
s.d.			4.9		12.8		14.0		5.2		1.6
Class III											
005	40	2	5.0	14	35.0	18	45.0	4	10.0	2	5.0
007	56	0	0.0	3	5.4	35	62.5	17	30.4	1	1.8
006	40	0	0.0	3	7.5	29	72.5	6	15.0	2	5.0
033	56	4	7.1	29	51.8	19	33.9	3	5.4	1	1.8
mean			3.0		24.9		53.5		15.2		3.4
s.d.			3.1		19.4		15.0		9.4		1.6

Table 4. Variants of (u) used by adults

Class I Speaker	Total tokens	(u–1) no.	%	(u–2) no.	%	(u–3) no.	%	(u–4) no.	%
015	40	22	55.0	16	40.0	2	5.0	0	0.0
050	38	17	44.7	20	52.6	1	2.6	0	0.0
030	40	24	60.0	14	35.0	2	5.0	0	0.0
045	40	26	65.0	14	35.0	0	0.0	0	0.0
mean			56.2		40.7		3.2		0.0
s.d.			7.5		7.2		2.1		0.0
Class IIa									
010	40	6	15.0	24	60.0	10	25.0	0	0.0
028	40	4	10.0	18	45.0	17	42.5	1	2.5
019	40	18	45.0	18	45.0	4	10.0	0	0.0
036	40	2	5.0	24	60.0	13	32.5	1	2.5
mean			18.8		52.5		27.5		1.3
s.d.			15.6		7.5		11.9		1.3
Class IIb									
032	40	0	0.0	7	17.5	18	45.0	15	37.5
040	40	1	2.5	15	37.5	17	42.5	7	17.5
023	40	0	0.0	20	50.0	20	50.0	0	0.0
047	40	0	0.0	13	32.5	19	47.5	8	20.0
mean			0.6		34.4		46.3		18.8
s.d.			1.1		11.6		2.8		13.3
Class III									
027	40	0	0.0	13	32.5	14	35.0	13	32.5
048	40	0	0.0	4	10.0	14	35.0	22	55.0
044	40	0	0.0	5	12.5	24	60.0	11	27.5
055	20	0	0.0	3	15.0	10	50.0	7	35.0
mean			0.0		17.5		45.0		37.5
s.d.			0.0		8.8		10.6		10.5

Table 5. Variants of (u) used by 15-year-olds

Class I	Total	(u–1)		(u–2)		(u–3)		(u–4)	
Speaker	tokens	no.	%	no.	%	no.	%	no.	%
004	40	8	20.0	24	60.0	8	20.0	0	0.0
049	40	3	7.5	20	50.0	13	32.5	4	10.0
031	22	13	59.1	7	31.8	2	9.1	0	0.0
037	40	13	32.5	25	62.5	2	5.0	0	0.0
mean			29.8		51.1		16.7		2.5
s.d.			19.1		12.1		10.7		4.3
Class IIa									
011	40	1	2.5	22	55.0	16	40.0	1	2.5
029	40	3	7.5	12	30.0	19	47.5	6	15.0
020	32	13	40.6	18	56.3	1	3.1	0	0.0
051	22	0	0.0	10	45.5	7	31.8	5	22.7
mean			12.7		46.7		30.6		10.1
s.d.			16.4		10.5		16.8		9.3
Class IIb									
024	30	0	0.0	1	3.3	14	46.7	15	50.0
026	40	2	5.0	12	30.0	19	47.5	7	17.5
025	40	0	0.0	6	15.0	20	50.0	14	35.0
052	12	0	0.0	6	50.0	6	50.0	0	0.0
mean			1.3		24.6		48.5		25.6
s.d.			2.2		17.5		1.5		18.7
Class III									
001	28	6	21.4	5	17.9	10	35.7	7	25.0
041	36	0	0.0	2	5.6	18	50.0	16	44.4
002	40	2	5.0	8	20.0	18	45.0	12	30.0
042	18	0	0.0	0	0.0	7	38.9	11	61.1
mean			6.6		10.9		42.4		40.1
s.d.			0.8		8.4		5.5		14.1

Table 6. Variants of (u) used by 10-year-olds

Class I	Total	(u–1)		(u–2)		(u–3)		(u–4)	
Speaker	tokens	no.	%	no.	%	no.	%	no.	%
009	40	11	27.5	23	57.5	6	15.0	0	0.0
021	40	10	25.0	17	42.5	12	30.0	1	2.5
022	40	4	10.0	18	45.0	16	40.0	2	5.0
046	40	18	45.0	19	47.5	3	7.5	0	0.0
mean			26.9		48.1		23.1		1.9
s.d.			12.4		5.7		12.7		2.1
Class IIa									
013	40	0	0.0	22	55.0	17	42.5	1	2.5
014	30	4	13.3	12	40.0	12	40.0	2	6.7
008	34	2	5.9	8	23.5	17	50.0	7	20.6
012	34	4	11.8	12	35.3	17	50.0	1	2.9
mean			7.8		38.5		45.6		8.2
s.d.			5.3		11.3		4.5		7.4
Class IIb									
018	40	3	7.5	10	25.0	17	42.5	10	25.0
035	40	0	0.0	7	17.5	17	42.5	16	40.0
016	40	0	0.0	14	35.0	18	45.0	8	20.0
053	40	0	0.0	9	22.5	17	42.5	14	25.0
mean			1.9		25.0		43.1		30.0
s.d.			3.3		6.4		1.1		7.9
Class III									
005	34	0	0.0	8	23.5	13	38.2	13	38.2
007	40	0	0.0	12	30.0	18	45.0	10	15.0
006	30	1	3.3	5	16.7	16	53.3	8	26.7
033	40	0	0.0	8	20.0	23	57.5	9	22.5
mean			0.8		22.6		48.5		28.1
s.d.			1.4		4.9		7.5		6.0

Table 7. Variants of (au) used by adults

Class I Speaker	Total tokens	(au–1) no.	%	(au–2) no.	%	(au–3) no.	%	(au–4) no.	%
015	40	12	30.0	19	47.5	9	22.5	0	0.0
050	24	6	25.0	17	70.8	1	4.2	0	0.0
030	40	21	52.5	17	42.5	2	5.0	0	0.0
045	40	37	92.5	3	7.5	0	0.0	0	0.0
mean			50.0		42.1		7.9		0.0
S.D.			26.6		22.7		8.6		0.0
Class IIa									
010	40	3	7.5	17	42.5	15	37.5	5	12.5
028	40	4	10.0	9	22.5	15	37.5	12	30.0
019	34	10	29.4	16	47.1	8	23.5	0	0.0
036	20	0	0.0	11	55.0	9	45.0	0	0.0
mean			11.7		41.8		35.9		10.6
S.D.			10.9		12.0		7.8		12.3
Class IIb									
032	40	0	0.0	3	7.5	22	55.0	15	37.5
040	40	0	0.0	4	10.0	14	35.0	22	55.0
023	32	0	0.0	3	9.4	15	46.9	14	43.8
047	40	0	0.0	5	12.5	18	45.0	17	42.5
mean			0.0		9.8		45.5		44.7
S.D.			0.0		1.8		7.1		6.4
Class III									
027	40	0	0.0	2	5.0	14	35.0	24	60.0
048	38	0	0.0	0	0.0	15	39.5	23	60.5
044	32	0	0.0	1	3.1	7	21.9	24	75.0
055	22	0	0.0	1	4.6	5	22.7	16	72.7
mean			0.0		3.2		29.8		67.1
S.D.			0.0		2.0		7.6		6.9

Table 8. Variants of (au) used by 15-year-olds

Class I		(au–1)		(au–2)		(au–3)		(au–4)	
Speaker	Total tokens	no.	%	no.	%	no.	%	no.	%
004	28	0	0.0	11	39.3	14	50.0	3	10.7
049	40	2	5.0	18	45.0	15	37.5	5	12.5
031	36	8	22.2	17	47.2	8	22.2	3	8.3
037	40	6	15.0	22	55.0	8	20.0	4	10.0
mean			10.6		46.6		32.4		10.4
S.D.			8.6		5.6		12.2		1.5
Class IIa									
011	40	0	0.0	15	37.5	21	52.5	4	10.0
029	36	0	0.0	9	25.0	17	47.2	10	27.8
020	24	8	33.3	9	37.5	7	29.2	0	0.0
051	26	0	0.0	0	0.0	8	30.8	18	69.2
mean			8.3		25.0		39.9		26.8
S.D.			14.4		15.3		10.1		26.5
Class IIb									
024	26	0	0.0	2	7.7	7	26.9	17	65.4
026	40	0	0.0	4	10.0	17	42.5	19	47.5
025	40	0	0.0	3	7.5	18	45.0	19	47.5
052	24	0	0.0	1	4.2	8	33.3	15	62.5
mean			0.0		7.3		36.9		55.7
S.D.			0.0		2.1		7.2		8.3
Class III									
001	30	0	0.0	1	3.3	10	33.3	19	63.3
041	30	0	0.0	2	6.7	14	46.7	14	46.7
002	38	0	0.0	4	10.5	24	63.2	10	26.3
042	34	0	0.0	1	2.9	16	47.1	17	50.0
mean			0.0		5.9		47.6		46.6
S.D.			0.0		3.1		10.6		13.3

Table 9. Variants of (au) used by 10-year-olds

Class I	Total	(au–1)		(au–2)		(au–3)		(au–4)	
Speaker	tokens	no.	%	no.	%	no.	%	no.	%
009	36	3	8.3	10	27.8	15	41.7	8	22.2
021	40	10	25.0	21	52.5	8	20.0	1	2.5
022	40	1	2.5	11	27.5	19	47.5	9	22.5
046	40	4	10.0	29	72.5	7	17.5	0	0.0
mean			11.5		45.1		31.7		11.8
S.D.			8.3		18.8		13.1		10.6
Class IIa									
013	40	0	0.0	13	32.5	22	55.0	5	12.5
014	40	1	2.5	14	35.0	19	47.5	6	15.0
008	26	0	0.0	8	30.8	14	53.9	4	15.4
012	40	1	2.5	19	47.5	20	50.0	0	0.0
mean			1.3		36.4		51.6		10.7
S.D.			1.3		6.6		3.0		6.3
Class IIb									
018	30	0	0.0	3	10.0	18	60.0	9	30.0
035	40	0	0.0	11	27.5	18	45.0	11	27.5
016	40	1	2.5	8	20.0	24	60.0	7	17.5
053	40	0	0.0	1	2.5	14	35.0	25	62.5
mean			0.6		15.0		50.0		34.4
S.D.			1.1		9.5		10.6		16.9
Class III									
005	30	0	0.0	0	0.0	3	10.0	27	90.0
007	40	0	0.0	7	17.5	15	37.5	18	45.0
006	32	0	0.0	6	18.8	24	75.0	2	6.3
033	24	0	0.0	0	0.0	8	33.3	16	66.7
mean			0.0		9.1		39.0		52.0
S.D.			0.0		9.1		23.3		30.8

Table 10. Variants of (a) used by adults

Class I	Total	(a–1)		(a–2)		(a–3)	
Speaker	tokens	no.	%	no.	%	no.	%
015	40	22	55.0	18	45.0	0	0.0
050	40	23	57.5	17	42.5	0	0.0
030	40	30	75.0	10	25.0	0	0.0
045	40	32	80.0	8	20.0	0	0.0
mean			66.9		33.1		0.0
s.d.			10.8		10.8		0.0
Class IIa							
010	40	11	27.5	28	70.0	1	2.5
028	40	1	2.5	33	82.5	6	15.0
019	40	13	32.5	27	67.5	0	0.0
036	40	9	22.5	31	77.5	0	0.0
mean			21.3		74.4		4.4
s.d.			11.4		6.0		6.2
Class IIb							
032	40	0	0.0	16	40.0	24	60.0
040	40	0	0.0	13	32.5	27	67.5
023	36	0	0.0	17	47.2	19	52.8
047	40	0	0.0	16	40.0	24	60.0
mean			0.0		39.9		60.1
s.d.			0.0		5.2		5.2
Class III							
027	40	0	0.0	15	37.5	25	62.5
048	40	0	0.0	15	37.5	25	62.5
044	36	0	0.0	14	38.9	22	61.1
055	36	0	0.0	17	47.2	19	52.8
mean			0.0		40.3		59.7
s.d.			0.0		4.1		4.1

Table 11. Variants of (a) used by 15-year-olds

Class I	Total	(a–1)		(a–2)		(a–3)	
Speaker	tokens	no.	%	no.	%	no.	%
004	32	9	28.1	23	71.9	0	0.0
049	40	6	15.0	30	75.0	4	10.0
031	40	25	62.5	15	37.5	0	0.0
037	40	17	42.5	20	50.0	3	7.5
mean			37.0		58.6		4.4
s.d.			17.6		15.5		4.5
Class IIa							
011	38	5	13.2	26	68.4	7	18.4
029	40	2	5.0	18	45.0	20	50.0
020	38	16	42.1	22	57.9	0	0.0
051	34	5	14.7	25	73.5	4	11.8
mean			18.7		61.2		20.1
s.d.			14.0		10.9		18.5
Class IIb							
024	26	0	0.0	13	50.0	13	50.0
026	40	9	22.5	20	50.0	11	27.5
025	44	2	4.6	28	63.6	14	31.8
052	40	0	0.0	26	65.0	14	35.0
mean			6.8		57.2		36.1
s.d.			9.3		7.2		8.5
Class III							
001	34	1	2.9	18	52.9	15	44.1
041	32	0	0.0	15	46.9	17	53.1
002	34	0	0.0	13	38.2	21	61.8
042	24	1	4.2	7	29.2	16	66.7
mean			1.8		41.8		56.4
s.d.			1.8		9.4		9.2

Table 12. Variants of (a) used by 10-year-olds

Class I	Total	(a–1)		(a–2)		(a–3)	
Speaker	tokens	no.	%	no.	%	no.	%
009	38	14	36.8	24	63.2	0	0.0
021	40	12	30.0	25	62.5	3	7.5
022	42	13	31.0	22	52.4	7	16.7
046	54	13	24.1	41	75.9	0	0.0
mean			30.5		63.5		6.0
s.d.			4.5		8.4		6.9
Class IIa							
013	44	15	34.1	27	61.4	2	4.6
014	44	13	29.6	29	65.9	2	4.6
008	40	15	37.5	23	57.5	2	5.0
012	40	16	40.0	24	60.0	0	0.0
mean			35.3		61.2		3.5
s.d.			3.9		3.1		2.0
Class IIb							
018	44	1	2.4	22	59.5	21	47.7
035	40	1	2.5	31	77.5	8	20.0
016	42	1	2.4	25	59.5	16	38.1
053	40	1	2.5	23	57.5	16	40.0
mean			2.4		61.1		36.5
s.d.			0.1		10.1		10.2
Class III							
005	44	3	6.8	26	59.1	15	34.1
007	40	0	0.0	23	57.5	17	42.5
006	40	1	2.5	21	52.5	18	45.0
033	42	2	4.8	29	69.1	11	26.2
mean			3.5		59.5		37.0
s.d.			2.5		6.0		7.4

Table 13. Percentage of glottal stops used by adults

Class I Speaker	Total tokens	/——C gs/no.	%	/——V gs/no.	%	/——# gs/no.	%
015	78	25/36	69.4	12/32	37.5	0/10	0.0
050	80	23/44	52.3	1/30	3.3	1/6	16.7
030	78	19/30	63.3	10/36	27.8	1/12	8.3
045	80	21/40	52.5	1/36	2.8	0/4	0.0
mean			59.4		17.9		6.3
S.D.			7.3		15.2		6.9
Class IIa							
010	80	20/24	83.3	12/28	42.9	10/28	35.7
028	78	23/26	88.5	26/38	68.4	4/14	28.6
019	78	27/40	67.5	0/30	0.0	0/8	0.0
036	80	33/36	91/7	17/34	50.0	0/10	0.0
mean			82.7		40.3		16.1
S.D.			9.3		25.1		16.3
Class IIb							
032	78	15/16	93.8	33/42	78.6	20/20	100.0
040	78	44/48	91.7	20/26	76.9	4/4	100.0
023	78	17/20	85.0	36/42	85.7	11/16	68.8
047	78	33/36	91.7	28/36	77.8	2/6	33.3
mean			90.5		79.8		75.5
S.D.			3.3		3.5		27.5
Class III							
027	80	26/28	92.9	33/34	97.1	15/18	83.3
048	78	31/32	96.9	32/36	88.9	10/10	100.0
044	80	37/38	97.4	27/36	75.0	6/6	100.0
055	78	37/38	97.4	26/30	86.7	9/10	90.0
mean			96.1		86.9		93.3
S.D.			1.9		7.9		7.1

Table 14. Percentage of glottal stops
used by 15-year-olds

Class I	Total	/——C		/——V		/——#	
Speaker	tokens	gs/no.	%	gs/no.	%	gs/no.	%
004	78	16/24	66.7	12/36	33.3	6/18	33.3
049	79	22/32	68.8	8/31	25.8	1/16	6.3
031	78	15/20	75.0	18/42	42.9	4/16	25.0
037	78	25/36	69.4	7/32	21.9	0/10	0.0
mean			70.0		31.0		16.2
s.d.			3.1		8.0		13.5
Class IIa							
011	80	28/30	93.3	25/28	89.3	21/22	95.5
029	78	21/22	95.5	24/26	92.3	28/30	93.3
020	78	31/44	70.5	2/22	9.1	1/12	8.3
051	78	31/38	81.6	25/32	78.1	7/8	87.5
mean			85.2		67.2		71.2
s.d.			10.0		34.0		36.4
Class IIb							
024	78	22/24	91.7	34/36	94.4	14/18	77.8
026	79	20/20	100.0	34/40	85.0	14/19	73.7
025	78	24/26	92.3	25/34	73.5	9/18	50.0
052	76	24/28	85.7	31/34	91.2	13/14	92.9
mean			92.4		86.0		73.6
s.d.			5.1		8.0		15.4
Class III							
001	74	27/28	96.4	22/24	91.7	22/22	100.0
041	78	35/36	97.2	32/34	94.1	8/8	100.0
002	76	24/24	100.0	26/30	86.7	22/24	91.7
042	78	36/36	100.0	32/32	100.0	10/10	100.0
mean			98.4		93.1		97.9
s.d.			1.6		4.8		3.6

Table 15. Percentage of glottal stops
used by 10-year-olds

Class I	Total	/——C		/——V		/——#	
Speaker	tokens	gs/no.	%	gs/no.	%	gs/no.	%
001	74	22/28	78.6	17/28	60.7	12/22	54.5
021	80	18/18	100.0	18/36	50.0	16/26	61.5
022	78	21/26	80.0	22/34	64.7	15/18	83.3
046	78	31/42	73.8	10/24	41.7	5/12	41.7
mean			83.3		54.3		60.3
S.D.			10.0		9.1		15.1
Class IIa							
013	78	26/30	86.7	26/30	86.7	16/18	88.9
014	78	39/44	88.6	21/22	95.5	11/12	91.7
008	80	18/20	90.0	28/34	82.4	23/26	88.5
012	78	37/44	84.1	16/24	66.7	8/10	80.0
mean			87.4		82.8		87.3
S.D.			2.2		10.4		4.4
Class IIb							
018	80	26/26	100.0	35/42	83.3	11/12	91.7
035	80	27/32	84.4	20/38	52.6	5/10	50.0
016	78	35/36	97.2	28/32	87.5	10/10	100.0
053	80	35/40	87.5	25/28	89.3	11/12	91.7
mean			92.3		78.2		83.3
S.D.			6.5		14.9		19.5
Class III							
005	80	22/24	91.7	33/38	86.8	18/18	100.0
007	78	26/26	100.0	33/36	91.7	13/16	81.3
006	78	35/36	97.2	15/18	83.3	20/24	83.3
033	78	22/24	91.7	25/36	69.4	16/18	88.9
mean			95.1		82.8		88.4
S.D.			3.6		8.3		7.3

Bibliography

Abercrombie, D. (1965) *Studies in Phonetics and Linguistics*. London: Oxford University Press.

Ballantyne, W. (1973) *A Survey of the Attitudes of Glasgow School-children in Forms III and IV*. Unpublished MEd thesis, University of Glasgow.

Baratz, Joan (1970) Educational considerations for teaching Standard English to Negro children, in *Teaching Standard English in the Inner City* (ed. R. W. Fasold & R. W. Shuy) pp.20-40. Washington, DC: Center for Applied Linguistics.

Barber, B. (1957) *Social stratification*. New York: Harcourt, Brace.

Barnes, D. (1971) Language in the secondary classroom, in *Language, the Learner and the School* (D. Barnes, J. Britton, H. Rosen and the LATE) revised ed., pp.9-77. Harmondsworth, Middx: Penguin Books.

Baubkus, L. & W. Viereck (1973) Recent American studies in socio-linguistics. *Archivum Linguisticum*, 103-11.

Berdan, R. (1976) *Numbers that count: analyzing variation in English vowels*. Paper read in the lecture series on Language Variation in America at the Linguistic Institute, Oswego, New York, 18 August 1976.

Bernstein, B. (1973) *Class, Codes and Control*. St Albans: Paladin.

Brennan, T. (1959) *Reshaping a City*. House of Grant.

Brooks, Charlotte K. (1964) Some approaches to teaching English as a second language, in *Non-standard Speech and The Teaching of English* (ed. W. A. Stewart) pp.24-32. Washington, DC: Center for Applied Linguistics.

Bullock, Sir Alan, chairman (1975) *A Language for Life*. London: HMSO.

Catford, J. C. (1957a) Vowel-system of Scots dialects. *Trans. Philol. Soc.*, 107-17.

—(1957b) The linguistic survey of Scotland. *Orbis, VI*, 105-21.

Cazden, C. B. (1971) Language programs for young children, notes from England and Wales, in *Language Training in Early Childhood Education* (ed. C. S. Lavatelli) pp.119-53. Urbana, Ill.: University of Illinois Press.

Centers, R. (1949) *The Psychology of Social Classes*. Princeton: Princeton University Press.

Chomsky, Carol (1969) *The Acquistition of Syntax in Children from 5 to 10*. Cambridge, Mass.: MIT Press.

Church, J. (1961) *Language and the Discovery of Reality*. New York: Random House.

Creber, J. W. P. (1972) *Lost for Words: language and educational failure*. Harmondsworth, Middx: Penguin Books.

Crystal, D. (1971a) *Linguistics*. Harmondsworth, Middx: Penguin Books.

—(1971b) Prosodic and paralinguistic correlates of social categories, in *Social Anthropology and Language* (ed. E. Ardener) pp.185-206. London: Tavistock Publications.

Davie, R., N. Butler & H. Goldstein (1972) *From Birth to Seven: a report of the National Child Development Study*. London: Longman.

Fasold, R. W. (1972) *Tense-Marking in Black English*. Arlington, Va: Center for Applied Linguistics.

Ford, J. (1969) *Social class and the Comprehensive School*. London: Routledge and Kegan Paul.

Freire, P. (1972) *Cultural Action for Freedom*. Harmondsworth, Middx: Penguin Books.

Frender, R. & W. E. Lambert (1973) Speech style and scholastic success, in *Georgetown Monograph on Language and Linguistics*, no.15, pp.237-71. Washington, DC: Georgetown University Press.

Giles, H. (1970) Evaluative reactions to accents. *Education Rev.*, *22*, 211-27.

—(1971) Patterns of evaluation to RP, South Welsh and Somerset accented speech. *Br. J. soc. and clin. Psychol.*, *10*, 280-1.

Gimson, A. C. (1962) *An Introduction to the Pronunciation of English*. London: Arnold.

Goldthorpe, J. H., D. Lockwood, F. Bechhofer & J. Platt (1969) *The Affluent Worker in the Class Structure*. London: Cambridge University Press.

Grant, W. (1931) *The Scottish National Dictionary*, vol. 1. Edinburgh: The Scottish National Dictionary Assoc. Ltd.

Grant, W. & Elizabeth H. A. Robson (1926) *Speech Training for Scottish Students*. London: Cambridge University Press.

Grieve, R. & D. J. Robertson (1964) *The City and the Region*. University of Glasgow Social and Economic Studies, Occasional Paper 2. Oliver and Boyd.

Hanley, C. (1958) *Dancing in the Streets*. Paisley: UR Books.

Hart, R. (1968) *The Comprehensive Development Area*. University of Glasgow Social and Economic Studies, Occasional Paper 9. Oliver and Boyd.

Harvey, B. (1968) *The Scope of Oracy: teaching spoken English*. London: Pergamon Press.

Jones, D. (1950) *The Pronunciation of English*, 3rd ed. London: Cambridge University Press.

Kellas, J. G. (1968) *Modern Scotland*. New York: Praeger.

Labov, W. (1963) The social motivation of a sound change. *Word*, *19*, 273-309.

—(1966a) *The Social Stratification of English in New York City*. Washington, DC: Center for Applied Linguistics.

—(1966b) Hypercorrection by the lower middle class as a factor in linguistic change, in *Sociolinguistics* (ed. W. Bright) pp.84-113. The Hague: Mouton.

—(1969) The logic of non-standard English. *Georgetown Monograph on Languages and Linguistics*, no.18, pp.1-22. Washington, DC: Georgetown University Press.

Lambert, W. E., R. C. Hodgson, R. C. Gardner & S. Fillenbaum (1960) Evaluational reactions to spoken language. *J. abnormal and soc. Psychol.*, *60*, 44-51.

Lenneberg, E. H. (1967) *Biological Foundations of Language*. London: Wiley.

Little, A. & J. Westergaard (1964) The trend of class differentials in educational opportunity. *Br. J. Sociol.*, *15*, 301-15.

Macaulay, R. K. S. (1973) Double standards. *Am. Anthrop.*, *75*, 1324-37.

—(1976) Social class and language in Glasgow. *Language in Society*, *5*, 173-88.

—& G. D. Trevelyan (1973) Language, education, and employment in Glasgow. (Report to the Social Science Research Council.) Edinburgh: Scottish Council for Research in Education.

McAllister, Anne H. (1963) *A Year's Course in Speech Training*, 9th ed. London: University of London Press.

Mackay, C. (1882) *The Poetry and Humour of the Scottish Language*. Paisley: Alexander Gardner.

Miller, R. & J. Tivy (1959) *The Glasgow Region*. British Association for the Advancement of Science Publications.

Oakley, C. A. (1967) *The Second City*. Glasgow: Blackie.

Parkin, F. (1971) *Class Inequality and Political Order*. New York: Praeger.

Patrick, J. (1973) *A Glasgow Gang Observed*. London: Eyre Methuen.

Piaget, J. (1959) *The Language and Thought of the Child*. London: Routledge and Kegan Paul.

Riddell, G. & D. Gulland (1975) *Teaching—Active or Passive*. Edinburgh: Holmes McDougall.

Romaine, Suzanne (1975) *Linguistic Variability in the Speech of some Edinburgh Schoolchildren*. Unpublished MLitt thesis, University of Edinburgh.

Rosen, C. & H. Rosen (1973) *The Language of Primary School Children*. Harmondsworth, Middx: Penguin Books.

Rosen, H. (1971) Towards a language policy across the curriculum, in *Language, the Learner and the School* (D. Barnes, J. Britton, H. Rosen and the LATE) revised ed., pp.117-68. Harmondsworth, Middx: Penguin Books.

Schutz, A. (1962) *Collected Papers: I. The Problem of Social Reality*. The Hague: Nijhoff.

Sledd, J. (1969) Bidialectalism: the politics of white supremacy. *English J.*, *58*, 1307-15, 1329.

—(1972) Doublespeak: dialectology in the service of Big Brother. *College English*, *33*, 439-56.

Speitel, H. H. (1973) *Dialect* (mimeo.). Paper delivered to the Seminar on Language and Learning, Scottish Council for Research in Education, Edinburgh, February.

The Guardian, 8, 9, 10 May 1973. The Struggle for Our Cities.

Time Magazine, 14 May 1973. Glasgow: The Meanest City.

Tough, Joan (1973) *Focus on Meaning*. London: Allen and Unwin.

Trudgill, P. J. (1971) *The Social Differentiation of English in Norwich*. Unpublished PHD dissertation, University of Edinburgh.

—(1972) Sex, covert prestige and linguistic change in the urban English of Norwich. *Language in Society*, *1*, 179-95.

—(1974) *Sociolinguistics: an introduction*. Harmondsworth, Middx: Penguin Books.

—(1975) Review of Bernstein (1973). *J. Linguistics*, *11*, 147-51.

Williams, Irene F. (1912) *Phonetics for Scottish Students: the sounds of polite Scottish described and compared with those of polite English*. Glasgow: James MacLehose and Sons.

Winston, Millicent (1971) *Some Aspects of the Pronunciation of Educated Scots*. Unpublished MLitt thesis, University of Edinburgh.

Wolfram, W. A. (1969) *A Sociolinguistic Description of Detroit Negro Speech*. Washington, DC: Center for Applied Linguistics.

179

PE 2274 .G57 M3 1977
Macaulay, Ronald K. S.
Language, social class, and
 education